Murray, Thomas Boyles

Pitcairn

The Island, the people and the pastor

Murray, Thomas Boyles

Pitcairn

The Island, the people and the pastor

Inktank publishing, 2018

www.inktank-publishing.com

ISBN/EAN: 9783747781135

PITCAIRN:

'HE ISLAND, THE PEOPLE, AND THE PASTOR;

WITH A SHORT ACCOUNT OF

The Mutiny of the Bounty.

BY THE

REV. THOS. BOYLES MURRAY, M.A.

SECRETARY OF THE SOCIETY FOR PROMOTING CHRISTIAN KNOWLEDGE.

"It was a chosen plot of fertile land,
Amongst wide waves set like a little nest,
As if it had by Nature's cunning hand
Been choicely picked out from all the rest,
And laid forth for ensample of the best."

SPENSER's *Faerie Queen*.

PUBLISHED UNDER THE DIRECTION OF
THE COMMITTEE OF GENERAL LITERATURE AND EDUCATION,
APPOINTED BY THE SOCIETY FOR PROMOTING
CHRISTIAN KNOWLEDGE.

SECOND EDITION.

LONDON:
Printed for the
SOCIETY FOR PROMOTING CHRISTIAN KNOWLEDGE;
SOLD AT THE DEPOSITORY,
GREAT QUEEN STREET, LINCOLN'S INN FIELDS;
4, ROYAL EXCHANGE; 16, HANOVER STREET, HANOVER SQUARE;
AND BY ALL BOOKSELLERS.

1853.

ADVERTISEMENT.

FROM the manner in which his little book has been already received, the Author is led to think that the additional intelligence respecting Pitcairn and the Islanders, which has reached him during the preparations for a Second Edition, will be interesting to the Reader.

July, 1853.

CONTENTS.

CHAPTER I.

CHAPTER II.

CHAPTER III.

CHAPTER IV.

CHAPTER V.

CHAPTER VI.

CHAPTER VII.

CHAPTER VIII.

CHAPTER IX.

ILLUSTRATIONS.

PREFACE

TO THE SECOND EDITION.

MUCH has been written about Pitcairn's Island; but the subject is a very fruitful one; and recent events have added greatly to the interest felt in the condition of the islanders. The arrival of their Pastor in England; his admission soon afterwards into holy orders; his desire to return, as speedily as possible, to the place of his choice; and, lastly, his interview with the Queen, and Prince Albert, to which he was graciously admitted two days previous to his quitting our shores; these things have brought to our minds the circumstances of Pitcairn, and its inhabitants, in a very striking manner.

The following letter addressed to the author of this work by Rear-Admiral Moresby, Commander-in-chief of her Majesty's naval

B

forces in the Southern Pacific, will explain the circumstances of Mr. Nobbs's visit to England:—

"Valparaiso, *August*, 1852.

"DEAR SIR,—This will be conveyed to you by Mr. Nobbs, the pastor of Pitcairn's Island. It was not until after our departure from thence, that I found he had received a letter from you, dated the 29th of November, 1850, which, I confess, has relieved me of much anxiety on the responsibility I have taken upon myself of sending Mr. Nobbs to England.

"I can most conscientiously assure you, that the state of society at Pitcairn has not been too highly described. The Bible and Prayer Book of 'the Bounty,' as handed to Mr. Nobbs from John Adams, have been, and continue to be, the objects of their study, and have enabled them to withstand the innovations, that too fervid imaginations, in America and elsewhere, have thought, by their correspondence, it was their calling to effect.

"The affectionate attachment of the islanders to Mr. Nobbs (who, in the triple capacity of pastor, surgeon, and teacher, is as necessary to them as their food,) created some little difficulty in his leaving; but it was overcome by the arrangement made for leaving with them our chaplain, Mr. Holman, and by my assurance that I would return their pastor to them with as little delay as possible. I hope I am not wrong in supposing that if Mr. Nobbs is found worthy of being ordained, only a short time will be required to prepare.

" I think I did not mention to the Bishop of London the way in which Mr. Nobbs reached Pitcairn. It disproves the malignant stories which have been circulated. And the success of twenty-four years' labour is an abundant proof that, under the blessing of God, he has educated in the principles of our Church, as one united family, a community whose simple and virtuous lives are so preeminent.

" In 1826, he left England for the purpose of going to Pitcairn. For nearly two years, by the way of the Cape of Good Hope, India, and Australia, he sought a passage. Finally, at Callao, in Peru, he met the owner of a launch, who, on the condition of Mr. Nobbs's fitting her out, agreed to accompany him to Pitcairn. Mr. Nobbs fitted her himself, and expended what little money he possessed. The owner was in ill health: nevertheless these two left Callao by themselves, on a voyage of 3,500 miles, which they accomplished in forty-two days. The owner died soon after their arrival. The launch was hauled on shore, and her materials used to build a house for Mr. Nobbs.

" I was four days on shore at Pitcairn, in constant discourse with the islanders. I am convinced that the time and the opportunity have arrived for giving them a minister of our Church; and that Mr. Nobbs is the person they wish, and the person at present best adapted for them.

" Believe me, truly yours,

" FAIRFAX MORESBY,

" REAR ADMIRAL."

REV. T. BOYLES MURRAY, M.A.

Amidst all the attentions which Mr. Nobbs received during his short sojourn in England, in the latter part of 1852, and which he truly appreciated, the thought of his flock at Pitcairn was evidently uppermost in his mind. Those who felt an interest in him, having heard of the virtuous habits and happy lives of the people, were less surprised at their pastor's wish to rejoin them, as soon as his errand was accomplished, that he might be again useful, more useful than before, and live and die among them. His connexion with the island is, however, of the nearest kind. His wife is living there, who is a grandaughter of Fletcher Christian; and they have eleven children.

The mention of Fletcher Christian reminds us of the origin of the present settlement at Pitcairn's Island. Without further anticipating, therefore, the eventful history which is connected with the place, and which proves that real life may be as romantic as fiction, the author will proceed to give an account of the island, and of the troublous times which preceded the pure and peaceful condition of this singular community.

Justly does it raise our wonder and gratitude to contemplate so exemplary a race, sprung from so guilty a stock. We hope and pray, that God's grace and blessing may remain upon this people; that no evil influence may come nigh to hurt them; and that they may still perceive and know religion to be the basis of their happiness. Then, happy Pitcairn, sea-girt isle! may you long continue a living model of all that is lovely, and of good report; and may nations not disdain to follow your example!

Lest it should be supposed by any reader, that the accounts of the present condition of the island are too delightful to be real, the author has thought it right to bring forward an array of testimony, in the shape of letters from living witnesses of unimpeachable credit, who have themselves visited the spot, and become personally acquainted with the people and the pastor.

The author feels that his cordial thanks are due to the many friends, who have favoured him with the loan of original manuscripts and drawings. It also gives him much satisfaction to acknowledge the courteous manner in which the authorities at the Admiralty complied with his request for particulars relating to the subject of his work.

67, Lincoln's Inn Fields, London,
June 1853.

PITCAIRN.

CHAPTER I.

THE BOUNTY — BREAD-FRUIT — OTAHEITE — FAREWELL TO OTAHEITE—THE MUTINY IN THE SHIP—MURDER OF JOHN NORTON AT TOFOA—SUFFERINGS AND ESCAPES OF BLIGH AND HIS COMPANY—FEEJEE ISLANDS—TIMOR—BATAVIA —ARRIVAL OF BLIGH AND ELEVEN OF HIS CREW IN ENGLAND—CAPTAIN, AFTERWARDS VICE-ADMIRAL, BLIGH.

In the year 1787 his Majesty's armed ship, *The Bounty*, was fitted out by the English government, the command being given to Lieutenant Bligh, to proceed to the South Sea islands for plants of the bread-fruit-tree, which afforded to the inhabitants of those islands, and of Otaheite especially, the greater portion of their food. This step was taken in consequence of representations made to King George the Third, by merchants and planters interested in his Majesty's West Indian possessions.

Lieutenant William Bligh, who was then about thirty-three years of age, had been sailing-master under Captain Cook, having been for four years with that great navigator in the *Resolution*. He was appointed in August, 1787, both commander and purser of the *Bounty*, which was stored and victualled for eighteen months. Besides this provision, he had supplies of portable soup, essence of meat, sour krout, and dried malt; to which were added some articles of iron and steel, trinkets, beads, and looking-glasses, for traffic with the natives. The plants, the best he could obtain, he was to convey to the West Indies, in order to attempt their growth for the support of the slave population; it having been the opinion of Sir Joseph Banks, who had visited Otaheite with Captain Cook in 1769, that the bread-fruit-tree might be successfully cultivated in those colonies.

The bread-fruit grows on a tree, which is about the size of a common oak, and, towards the top, divides into large and spreading branches. The leaves are of a very deep green. The fruit springs from twigs to the size of a penny loaf. It has a thick rind; and before becoming ripe, it is gathered, and baked in an oven, when the inner part is like

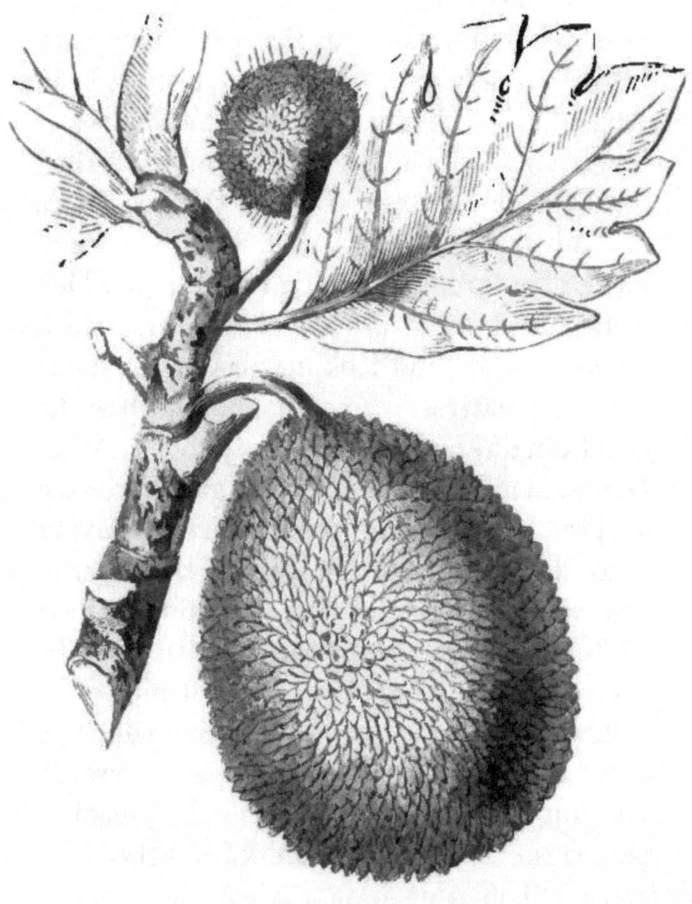

THE BREAD-FRUIT.

the crumb of wheaten bread, and found to be very nutritive. Captain Wm. Dampier,* who sailed round the world in the year 1688, described the bread-fruit as having "neither seed nor stone in the inside; but all is of pure substance like bread. It must be eaten new; for if it is kept above twenty-four hours, it grows harsh and choaky; but it is very pleasant before it is too stale. This fruit lasts in season eight months in the year, during which the natives of Guam eat no other sort of food of bread kind. I did never," says he, "see of this fruit anywhere but here. The natives told us that there is plenty of this fruit growing on the rest of the Ladrone Islands; and I did never hear of it anywhere else."

The *Bounty* of nearly 215 tons burden, left Spithead on the 23d of December, 1787, carrying forty-six persons, including the commander, and a botanist, and gardener. They started with a fresh breeze, easterly,

* An old English navigator, born in 1652, whose name is associated with that of the celebrated Alexander Selkirk, who sailed in company with him. Selkirk's wonderful adventures suggested to De Foe the idea of his inimitable Robinson Crusoe.

which moderated on the 25th, so that they were able to keep their Christmas with cheerfulness; but it increased to such a heavy gale by the 27th, that the vessel suffered damage; a sea which she shipped having broken some of the planks of the boats, and an azimuth compass. It also wetted and injured a few bags of bread in the cabin, which, when the weather improved, were got up, and dried. The voyage was attended with many circumstances of difficulty and danger. The few hours of respite from the hard westerly winds that blew, were, according to a fine expression in Lord Anson's voyage, like the elements drawing breath, to return upon them with redoubled violence. Having tried in vain, in a tempestuous ocean, to go by Cape Horn, they at last made a passage round the Cape of Good Hope; and having visited Van Diemen's Land, and New Zealand, the ship arrived at Otaheite, anchoring in Matavai Bay, at 10 in the forenoon of the 26th of October, 1788.

The voyagers were received with kindness by the natives, who asked after Captain Cook, Sir Joseph Banks, and others who had visited them some years before. But their first inquiries of the voyagers were, if they were *Tyos*, which signifies, friends; and whether they came from *Pretanie*, (Britain.) Having become satisfied on these two important points, they instantly crowded the deck in such numbers, that Bligh could scarcely find his own people. He had prepared and written down certain rules to be observed by all his men for facilitating a trade for provisions, and establishing a good understanding with the natives. Immediately on anchoring, these orders were stuck up on the mizen-mast. It was against the rules, to purchase curiosities, or provisions, except by application to a person duly appointed as a purveyor. With respect to curiosities, it appears that none struck the seamen so forcibly as a roasted pig, and some bread-fruit; and these came in abundance.

Having passed about six pleasant months in the island, and collected plants, the party took leave of their friends at Otaheite, and, after touching at Annamooka for water &c., put to sea again April 27, 1789. Bligh, in his "Voyage to the South Seas," published a plan and section of the *Bounty*, showing the manner of fitting and stowing the pots for receiving the bread-fruit plants. Of these plants he had 1,015.

It is probable that Bligh would have been spared much trouble and misery had he quitted Otaheite sooner; but he had been prevailed upon by the kindness of the chiefs to delay his departure; and during the interchange of friendly civilities, and hospitable receptions, both on board the *Bounty*, and on shore, three of the men belonging to the ship, of whom more will be said presently, deserted, taking with them the small cutter, a chest of fire-arms and ammunition. They were soon captured by Bligh, with the help of some of the natives at a neighbouring island, Tettaha. These three deserters wrote a letter of humble acknowledgment to their captain, for his clemency in not bringing them to trial, and promised good conduct in future: but they were very soon afterwards mutineers. Their letter was dated January 26th, 1789, three months before Bligh and his companions, with heavy hearts, bade farewell to charming Otaheite.

The reader will observe that the word, Otaheite, is here used, as spelt by Captain Cook. It is now often printed, Tahiti. In pronouncing it, the natives are accustomed first to draw in their breath: hence the sound as of a vowel at the beginning of the word.

On the arrival of the *Bounty* off Tofoa, one of the Friendly Islands, on the 28th of April, 1789, a dreadful mutiny broke out among some of the ship's officers and men, with Fletcher Christian, the master's mate, at their head. He was of a respectable family in the north of England, a young man of talent in his profession, twenty-four years of age, and of a quick and daring spirit.

It is very difficult, at this distance of time, to judge of the real motive or motives which actuated these men in their evil design. Indeed, at the period of the mutiny, the object which the leaders had in view could only be conjectured. Bligh gave it as his opinion, that they had flattered themselves with the hope of returning to Otaheite, and again leading the agreeable kind of life which they had passed in that island.

It was alleged on the other hand, that,

during the voyage, there had been frequent misunderstandings between the commander and Fletcher Christian; and that offence had been given by the former to Christian, and to some of the men, on the day before the mutiny. Much stress has been laid on each of these circumstances, as if one or the other had been the cause of the outrage.

On this part of the subject it is unnecessary to dwell; though it must not be wholly passed over. To assume, without proof, that the act of the mutineers was owing to tyranny on the part of Bligh, is surely not to make their case better; because, in this point of view, the deed must be looked upon as one, not only of sinful revenge against him, but of cruelty to their unoffending messmates. For what prospect was there to men exposed in such a manner to the horrors of the deep, but death, either by drowning or starvation?

It was natural for those who had been accomplices in the mutiny to excuse themselves as far as possible; but every thoughtful reader will weigh and examine the value of statements coming from such quarters.

Bligh was a thoroughbred sailor of a

former school. Notwithstanding the occasional ebullitions of anger and excitement, from the prevalence of which every one may well strive to keep his own heart with all diligence, still it was his study to make his men, not only efficient, but comfortable and happy. Attending strictly to his own duty, he deemed it his part to see that they should attend to theirs: and it will be allowed, that he had some men under his command intractable enough to try severely a temper less hasty than his. On the 9th of March, he had found it necessary, on a complaint of the master, to punish one of the seamen for insolence, and mutinous behaviour.

With regard to Christian, he says, "This was the third voyage he had made with me; and as I found it necessary to keep my ship's company at three watches, I had given him an order to take charge of the third, his abilities being thoroughly equal to the task."

Speaking of the division into three watches, he adds, "I have always considered this a desirable regulation, when circumstances will admit of it, on many accounts; and am persuaded that unbroken rest not only contributes much to the health of the ship's company, but enables them more readily to exert themselves in cases of sudden emergency."*

On the evening before the mutiny, Bligh invited Christian to supper in his cabin; an invitation which was declined. Christian had the watch for two hours. That night, the 27th of April, 1789, was remarked for its beauty, even in the tropical regions, all nature being calm and lovely around; but it was the eve of a day of consternation and terror.

Full of desperate intentions, Christian, at the next morning's watch, which was from 4 to 8, began to sound Matthew Quintal, and some others, and soon gained over the greater part of the men. Having rapidly arranged their plans, they got at the arms, under pretence of requiring a gun to shoot a shark, which was astern of the ship. At the dawn of day, they roughly awoke Bligh, who, starting up in amazement, on seeing men about him armed with cutlasses and pistols, called out loudly for assistance. On his

* Voyage to the South Sea, undertaken by command of his Majesty, &c., published by Bligh, in 1790, page 21.

demanding what they meant, "Hold your tongue, sir, or you are dead this instant," was the answer which he received. Some of the mutineers, among whom Christian, Churchill, Mills, and Burkitt, were the most active, with oaths, and violence, tied his hands with cords, behind his back, not giving him time to dress; and forcing him on to the deck in his shirt, kept him under a guard, behind the mizen-mast. The boatswain and others, having been compelled to hoist out the launch, Bligh and eighteen men were forced to go into her, and were quickly veered astern of the ship by a rope.

Besides Christian, and eight other mutineers, whose names will be mentioned in a future page, as afterwards settling at Pitcairn, the following remained in the *Bounty*:—Peter Heywood, midshipman; George Stewart, midshipman; James Morrison, boatswain's mate; Charles Churchill, master at arms; Matthew Thompson, John Sumner, Richard Skinner, Thomas Burkitt, John Millward, Thomas Ellison, Michael Byrne, seamen; Henry Hillbrant, cooper; William Musprat, commander's steward; Joseph Cole-

C

man, armourer; Charles Norman, carpenter's mate; Thomas M'Intosh, carpenter's crew; making twenty-five of the most able men in the ship.

The nineteen souls in the Launch were as follow: — WILLIAM BLIGH, commander; John Fryer, master; William Elphinston, master's mate; John Hallett, midshipman; Thomas Hayward, midshipman; Robert Tinkler, a boy; William Peckover, gunner; William Cole, boatswain; William Purcell, carpenter; Thomas D. Ledward, surgeon's mate; John Samuel, clerk and steward; David Nelson, botanist; Lawrence Labogue, sailmaker; Peter Linkletter, quarter-master; John Norton, quarter-master; George Simpson, quarter-master's mate; Thomas Hall, ship's cook; John Smith, commander's cook; Robert Lamb, butcher.

Having flung them a few pieces of pork, amounting to 32 pounds, 150 pounds of bread, 28 gallons of water, 6 quarts of rum, 6 bottles of wine, four cutlasses, a quadrant, and a compass, with a quantity of twine, canvass, and cordage, the mutineers sailed away. Christian, as if to keep up the courage of his comrades, and exert his usurped authority in the vessel, ordered a dram of spirits to be served to each. Little did they think, when shouting with joy at their miscalled liberty, what troubles they were bringing upon their own heads.

The party of men thus cast adrift on the wide ocean, were in a miserable condition. They began with touching at Tofoa, an island about thirty miles from the scene of the mutiny. There they landed and endeavoured to obtain bread-fruit, and water; but after some show of friendship, the natives who lined the beach, gave signs of violence by knocking stones together, which they had in each hand. Macca-ackavow, one of their chiefs, having in vain requested Bligh to remain that night, May 1, 1789, the treacherous old chief got up, and said, "Then, mattie," which signifies, We will kill you, and left him. Scarcely had the poor voyagers reached their boat, when about two hundred natives attacked them with stones, which flew like a shower of shot; and all would probably have been cut off by these savages, had not one of the crew, John Norton, quarter-master, run up the beach, for the purpose of releasing the boat. This brave man fell a sacrifice, in preserving the lives of his companions. He was surrounded by the natives, who barbarously murdered him, and afterwards beat him about the head with stones.

Poor Norton was a man of worthy character, who supported an aged parent out of his wages. They killed him on the beach, and dragged the body up the country to one of their *malais*, or lawns, and there left it exposed for two or three days before they buried it. This story was related by the islanders to Mr. William Mariner, when he visited Tofoa, eighteen years afterwards; and they added, that no grass had since grown on the line along which they had dragged the corpse, nor upon the spot where it had lain unburied. Such a tale induced him to make further examination; and he found a bare line, as they had stated, in a place where it would seem there was no frequency of passers by; and at the termination of the track, a bare spot, extending transversely, about the length and breadth of a man.

This anecdote is found in Mariner's Account

of the Natives of the Tonga Islands. It is not intended to give much weight to the story, there being many ways of explaining the seeming wonder. But a matter connected with one of the *Bounty* men, and so heroic a character too, deserves to be recorded in this place. Those who related the marvellous part of the account were of such a treacherous and deceitful race, that Mariner, in visiting the volcano on the summit of Tofoa, in company with a native guide, thought it necessary to provide himself with a pistol, as a defence against any violent measures on the part of his companion. Nor would he advance with him too near the crater of the volcano, "lest the man might have some sinister intent."*

After the murder of Norton, on the 1st of May, many of the natives in canoes followed Bligh's boat very quickly, and renewed the assault with stones of which they had brought a great quantity; but, being attracted by some clothes which were, by his order, thrown to them, and which they stopped to pick up, they lost time, and abandoned the pursuit.

It was then resolved by the party, at

* Mariner's "Tonga Islands," vol. i. chap. viii.

Bligh's instance, to make for a Dutch settlement on the island of Timor, a distance of no less than 3,618 miles.

The sufferings undergone by these eighteen men, in a boat only twenty-three feet in length, and six feet nine inches in breadth, heavily laden, and without any awning, were very severe. They had to encounter heavy storms, and the pains of cold and hunger. Aware of the vast tract of voyage before them, they promised to be content with one ounce of bread, and a quarter of a pint of water a day for each person.

The courageous and skilful manner in which Bligh pursued his course to the end, forms a striking fact in the annals of naval adventure. Having intreated the men, in the most solemn manner, not to depart from the promise which they had made, he, on the 2d of May, bore away, and shaped his course for New Holland, across a sea little explored. The boat was of such limited dimensions, that her gunwales are stated to have been not more than six inches above the water. In a violent tempest, which soon broke over them, the boat shipped such a quantity of water, that it was only by great exertions that she could be kept afloat.

On the 5th, continuing their course to the north-west, they saw and passed a cluster of islands. Hitherto they had not been able to keep any other account than by guess; but they had now succeeded in getting a log-line marked, and by a little practice some could count the seconds with a tolerable degree of exactness. The helpless and confined state in which they were, induced Mr. Bligh to put his crew to watch and watch, so that one half might be on the look-out, while the others lay down in the boat's bottom, or upon a chest. Even this gave but a trifling alleviation to their sufferings. Being exposed to constant wet and cold, and not having room to stretch their limbs, they became often so dreadfully cramped as to be incapable of moving them.

On the 7th another group of islands was seen, from whence they observed two large canoes in pursuit of them, one of which, at four o'clock in the afternoon, had arrived within two miles of the boat, when the savages gave up the chase, and returned to shore. Mr. Bligh concluded, from their direction, that these must have been the Feejee Islands.

The appearance of these islands, especially of the two largest, is generally very beautiful and interesting. They are well-wooded, and have extensive rivers. Little, however, is known respecting the interior: nor would it be safe to penetrate into the country without an armed party.

The late Captain Worth, who visited the Feejee islands in the *Calypso* in 1848, said in a report which he sent home, that the group, containing a very large population, may be conveniently divided into three parts, the Central, the Windward, and the Leeward islands.

Bligh, in his defenceless state, appears to have had a fortunate escape from the Feejeeans, who are not only cunning, cruel, and vindictive, but are to be ranked among the vilest cannibals. This horrid custom of theirs is the more remarkable, as they excel their neighbours in talent and ingenuity, of which Captain Cook saw several specimens in 1777, and which have been noticed by subsequent travellers. Cannibalism prevails everywhere among them, except in the places in which Christianity has made progress. Captain Worth was informed by Mr. Hunt, the chairman of the Wesleyan Mission, that not fewer than five hundred persons had been eaten within fifteen miles of his residence, during the five years previous. Many of the Feejeeans acknowledge that they greatly prefer human flesh to any animal food whatever. Much more might be said on the frightful traits of character which have been drawn of these people. But it is time to return to the band of men who had, up to that time, been wonderfully preserved from threatening dangers.

A small blank book, which had been commenced in the *Bounty*, for the insertion of signals, was now found very serviceable in the launch. This book was used by Bligh, who, in consequence of its exposure to the wet, found it difficult to make his notes. "It is with the utmost difficulty," he says, "that I can open a book to write; and I feel truly sensible I can do no more than point out where these lands are to be found, and give some idea of their extent." This affecting document is in existence, in the possession of his daughters, and is much blotted and weather-stained.

On the 8th, the weather was calm and fair, which gave the voyagers an opportunity of drying their clothes, and cleaning out the boat. Mr. Bligh also amused "all hands," by relating to them a description of New Guinea, and New Holland, and supplying them with every information in his power, that in case any fatal accident should happen to him, the survivors might be able to pursue their course to Timor; of which place they had before known nothing, except by name.

At this date the whole day's allowance to each was an ounce and a half of pork, half a pint of cocoa-nut milk, an ounce of bread and a tea-spoonful of rum. "Hitherto," says Bligh, "I had issued the allowance by guess; but I now made a pair of scales with two cocoa-nut shells; and having accidentally some pistol-balls in the boat, twenty-five of which weighed one pound, or sixteen ounces, I adopted one of these balls as the proportion of weight that each person

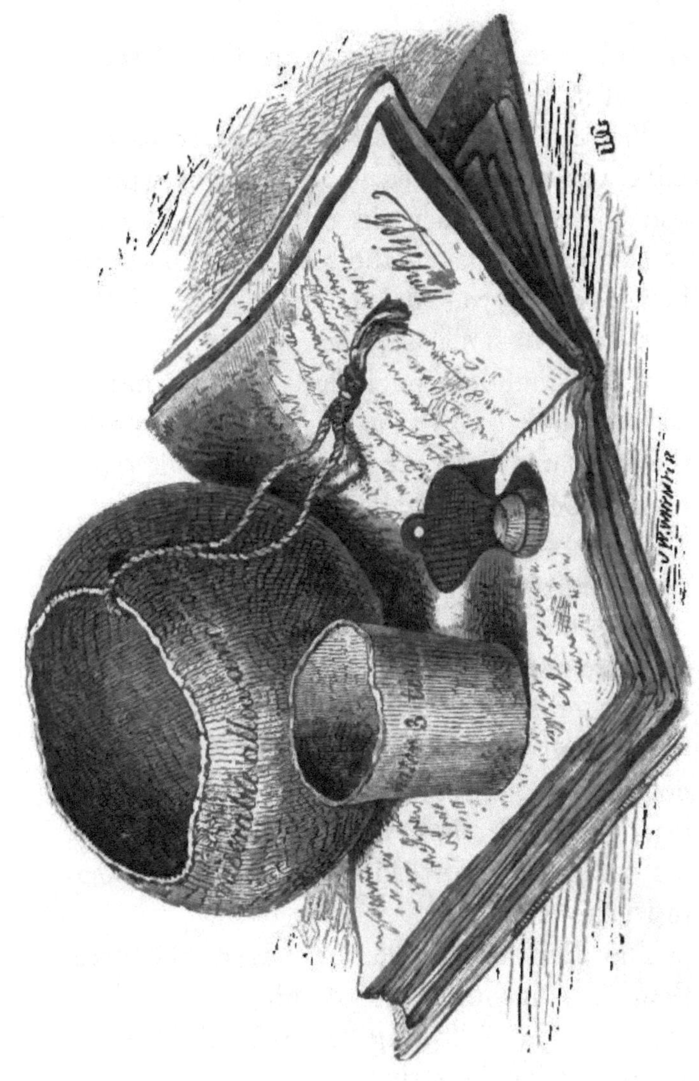

LIEUT. BLIGH'S GOURD, CUP, BULLET-WEIGHT, AND BOOK.

should receive of bread at the time I served it."

The allowance of half-a-pint of cocoa-nut milk was soon reduced to a quarter of a pint; and these poor men, in their deep distress, at last relished even the wetted and decayed bread, which was doled out to each in the most careful and scrupulous manner. A storm of thunder and lightning, with heavy rain, though it drenched them once more to the skin, was yet very acceptable, as it gave them about twenty gallons of water.

The annexed engraving, from a drawing made expressly for this work from the originals, shows the bowl, or gourd, out of which the commander took his meals; the bullet-weight; the little quarter-of-a-pint horn mug for serving out the water; and, though last, not the least interesting, Bligh's own boat-log-book. All these are much treasured by his daughters, who kindly permitted them to be sketched.

The diameter of the gourd is rather more than five inches: the depth nearly four inches. The following words are cut with a knife under the string,

W. Bligh, April, 1789.

Written in ink round the gourd:

The cup I eat my miserable allowance out of.

The horn cup is about two inches in depth, and not quite two inches in diameter. Round it are these words written in ink by Bligh:—

Allowance of water 3 *times a-day.*

The bullet is set in a small hasp-shaped metal plate, which Bligh afterwards used to wear suspended by a riband round his neck. Above the bullet are these words:—

This bullet, $\frac{1}{32}$ *of a lb. was the allowance of Bread which supported* 18 *men for* 48 *days, served to each person three times a-day.*

On the obverse:—

Under the command of Captain Will. Bligh from the 28*th April,* 1789, *to the* 14*th of June following.*

On the 10th the weather again began to be extremely boisterous, with constant rain, and frequent thunder and lightning. The sea was so rough, as often to break over the boat, so that they were constantly baling, and often in imminent danger of perishing. In addition to their other misfortunes, the bread was damaged by the salt-water. Their clothes being never dry, they derived no refreshment from the little rest they sometimes got. Many were benumbed and cramped by the cold, and afflicted with violent shiverings, and inward pains. As the weather still continued tempestuous, Mr. Bligh recommended all to take off their clothes, and wring them in the salt-water. This produced a warmth, which, whilst their clothing was wet with the rain they could not enjoy.

On the 24th it was thought necessary to reduce their already wretched pittance; and it was agreed that each person should receive one twenty-fifth part of a pound of bread for breakfast, and the same quantity for dinner, omitting the allowance for supper.

The next day they saw several noddies, and other sea-fowl, a few of which they were so fortunate as to catch; one of the birds came so near the boat, that it was caught by the hand. There was no wish to cook these birds. Besides the difficulty of dressing them, the claims of hunger were too peremptory to wait for such a process. Bligh divided one of them, which was of the size of a small pigeon, into eighteen portions; "and," says he, "by a well-known method at sea, of,

Who shall have this? it was distributed with the allowance of bread and water, for dinner, and eaten up, bones and all, with salt-water for sauce." The simple and impartial method alluded to is this:—One man turns his back on the several portions of food. Another points to one of these portions, saying, *Who shall have this?* He is answered by the former, who names one of the party; each having thus an equal chance of the best morsel. After they had shared this grand prize, several boobies flew near them in the evening, and they caught one of them. "This bird," says our narrator, "is as large as a duck. Like the noddy, it has received its name from seamen, for suffering itself to be caught on the masts and yards of ships." The sight of sea-birds indicated the neighbourhood of land. The weather was now dry and fine. But even this soon became distressing; the heat of the sun was so intense, that many of the people were seized with a languor and faintness, which made them weary of life.

On the morning of the 29th, breakers were discovered about a quarter of a mile distant; they immediately hauled off, and were soon out of danger. At daylight they saw the reefs over which the sea broke furiously. Steering along the edge of it, an opening was observed, through which the boat passed. They were then in smooth water; they tried to catch fish, and all their past hardships seemed to be forgotten. It occurred to Bligh, that they were within a few miles of Providential Channel. A small island within the reefs, he named, Island of Direction, as it served to show the entrance of the channel to which they had been conducted. At this happy period, he wrote, "We now returned God thanks for His gracious protection; and with much content took our miserable allowance of a twenty-fifth of a pound of bread, and a quarter of a pint of water for dinner."

They had the advantage of using frequently a devout and suitable prayer to God, which had been drawn up by their commander, partly from the Prayer-Book. This form of prayer, which is in Mr. Bligh's handwriting, in the manuscript book alluded to, includes an humble confession of sins on the part of those who were suffering under the Divine chastisement, invokes the Almighty's protection for the future, and contains a thanksgiving to Him, who ruleth the raging of the sea, and who had rescued these his afflicted creatures from the jaws of death.

The coast of New Holland now began to show itself distinctly. They landed in a fine sandy bay on an island near the main. Here they found plenty of oysters, water, and berries, which by men in their sad and reduced condition, were looked upon as luxuries. After a more comfortable repose than they had enjoyed for many nights, they were preparing the next day to depart, when about twenty natives, quite black, appeared on the opposite shore, running, hallooing, and making signs to land. Each was armed with a spear; several others were seen peeping over the tops of the adjacent hills. Bligh, who had earned some experience, and could judge of the nature of such overtures, judged it most prudent to make the best of his way to sea. He named the place, Restoration Island; as not only applicable to his own situation, but the anniversary of King Charles's Restoration, when it was discovered. As the boat sailed along the shore, many other parties of the natives came down, waving green boughs as a token of peace and friendship; but Mr. Bligh thought it wise not to land.

On the 31st, the voyagers landed on a small island, in order to get a distinct view of the coast, as well as to obtain food. Some of the men were sent for supplies, the others were ordered to remain in the boat. One of the former party, unwilling to work, said he would rather go without his dinner than have to search for it. The scene which followed was so remarkable that it must be told in Bligh's own words. "One person, in particular, went so far as to tell me, with a mutinous look, that he was as good a man as myself. It was not possible for me to judge where this might have an end, if not stopped in time: therefore, to prevent disputes in future, I determined either to preserve my command, or die in the attempt. Seizing a cutlass, I ordered him to take hold of another, and defend himself; on which he called out, that I was going to kill him, and immediately made concessions. I did not allow this to interfere with the harmony of the boat's crew, and everything soon became quiet."

One of the three men who had been sent to catch noddies, chose to proceed by himself, and disturbed the birds to such a degree, that only twelve were brought back by the party. This man, Robert Lamb, received a good beating from Bligh, for his folly and obstinacy; and he afterwards confessed, when at Java, that he had eaten nine birds raw, after he had separated from his two companions.

From this little island, after making hearty meals on birds and shell-fish, they again put to sea, steering along the shore, often touching at the different islands and sandy quays, to refresh themselves, and to get such supplies as could be afforded. On the evening of the 3d of June, they had passed, by a most difficult and dangerous passage, through Endeavour Straits, and were once more launched into the open ocean, shaping their course for the island of Timor. A continuance of wet and tempestuous weather, and incessant fatigue, affected even the strongest among them to such a degree, that they appeared to be almost at the point of death. Mr. Bligh then, as at other times, used every effort to revive their drooping spirits.

At three o'clock in the morning of the 12th of June, to their inexpressible joy, they discovered the island of Timor. Here Bligh breaks out in language which will find an echo in the heart of every reader, who has accompanied him in imagination, thus far in all his troubles and privations:—"It is not possible for me to describe the pleasure which the blessing of the sight of this land diffused among us. It appeared scarce credible to ourselves, that in an open boat, and so poorly provided, we should have been able to reach the coast of Timor in forty-one days after leaving Tofoa, having, in that time, run, by our log, a distance of 3,618 miles; and that, notwithstanding our extreme distress, no one should have perished in the voyage."

On the 13th they found land in a small sandy bay near the island of Roti, where the natives, who were of a dark tawny colour, received them courteously, bringing them a few pieces of dried turtle, and some ears of Indian corn, which were very acceptable. They offered to bring other refreshments; but Bligh, who acknowledged their kindness, and the "European politeness" of some of them, determined to push on. At ten o'clock that night, he issued for supper a double allowance of bread, and a little wine to each person; and at one the next morning, which was Sunday, "after the most sweet and happy sleep that ever men enjoyed," they weighed anchor, and continued along the east shore. Then, after rowing and resting alternately, for some distance, they were, on the 14th June, regaled with sounds and sights dear to every seaman, but almost transporting to those who had so long been strangers to all that was joyous in their profession. The report of two cannons that were fired, gave new life to all, and soon after they discovered two square-rigged vessels, and a cutter, at anchor to the eastward. Out of a bundle of signal flags, which the boatswain had thrown into the launch before they left the *Bounty*, they had made a small jack, which was hoisted in the main shrouds, as a signal of distress; "for," says Bligh, "I did not think proper to land without leave."

Soon after daybreak, at the Dutch settlement of Coupang, a soldier hailed them to land, and what was their delight, in making their way through a crowd of natives, who stood gazing upon their emaciated forms with wonder and pity, to meet with an ENGLISH SAILOR! This man, who belonged to one of the vessels in the road, at once told Bligh, that his Captain was the second person in the town of Coupang. To him the party were conducted; and certainly Captain Spikerman was a living example of the truth of the good old proverb, "A friend in need, is a friend indeed." He received them into his house, took care of them, and introduced them to the governor. They met with the most friendly and hospitable treatment from the governor, Mr. Adrian Van Este, though he was in a very ill state of health. He sent a message, regretting that his illness prevented his befriending them in person; but he committed them to the care of Mr. Wanjon, his son-in-law; who, with other leading persons at Coupang, rendered their situation comfortable. The picture given of the landing, displays in a striking manner the sad condition of these afflicted creatures, and the feelings excited in their preservers. "Our bodies were nothing but skin and bones; our limbs were full of sores, and we were clothed in rags. In this condition, with the tears of joy and gratitude flowing down our cheeks, the people of Timor beheld us with a mixture of horror, surprise, and pity."

On the 20th of July, Nelson, the botanist, died of fever. He was a man much respected, and of great scientific knowledge. He had been originally appointed to the *Bounty* on the recommendation of Sir Joseph Banks, to have the management of the bread-fruit plants, and had been similarly engaged in Captain Cook's last voyage.

On the 30th of August, Bligh, and his crew of sixteen, sailed from Coupang for Batavia, taking in tow the launch in which their lives had been so providentially preserved. After some detention at Batavia, in consequence of illness, he was able to sail homeward; and on the 14th of March, 1790, he landed at Portsmouth.

Of the eighteen who had been with him in the launch, eleven returned to their native country. He had brought all but Norton safe to Coupang: Elphinston, Linkletter, Hall, and Lamb, died soon afterwards. Ledward remained at Batavia.

A few words respecting Bligh will be interesting. It appears by the register of St. Andrew's, Plymouth, that William, son of Francis and Jane Bligh, was baptized at that church, Oct. 4th, 1754. The general residence of the family was near Bodmin.

After the Court-Martial on the mutineers, in 1792, Bligh was made a Commander, and then a Post Captain; the three years' service, according to regulation, being, in his case, dispensed with as a mark of favour.

Having been again employed to visit the South Seas, he fully succeeded in conveying the bread-fruit plant to the West Indies; and for this, in 1794, he received a gold medal from the Society of Arts.

In the same year he issued an answer to certain allegations, which had been published to his prejudice, and replied with much calmness to what he styled, "Mr. Edward Christian's defence of his brother." In the preface to his answer, which consists chiefly of original documents, by way of "proofs," he said; "One of the hardest cases which can befall any man is to be reduced to the necessity of defending his character by his own assertions only. As such fortunately is not my situation, I have rested my defence on the testimony of others, adding only such of the written orders issued by me in the course of the voyage as are connected with the matter in question; which orders, being issued publicly in writing, may be offered as evidence of unquestionable credit."

Bligh afterwards fought under Admiral Parker at the Dogger Bank, and under Lord Howe at Gibraltar.

In 1797, he commanded the *Director*, in Admiral Lord Duncan's fleet, at the famous battle of Camperdown. Miss Bligh has some drawings by Owen; one representing the *Director* coming up with the *Vrijheid*, the ship of the Dutch Admiral, De Winter; another showing the engagement between them; and the third, the *Vrijheid*, almost a hulk, silenced, and striking to the British flag.

In 1801, Bligh commanded the *Glatton*, at the battle of Copenhagen, under Lord Nelson, who, having sent for him after the action, publicly thanked him for his services.

In 1805 he was appointed Governor of New South Wales. The steps which he took, with a view to the benefit of the colony, in accordance with instructions laid down for him by the government at home,* occasioned much dissatisfaction to some parties on the spot, though his measures obtained the written approbation of his Majesty's Government.† In January, 1808, he was deposed at Sydney by the New South Wales Corps, headed by Lieut.-Colonel G. Johnston. In May 1811, Colonel Johnston was tried by Court-Martial at Chelsea Hospital, and was sentenced to be cashiered. The present Chief Baron of the Exchequer, then Mr. Pollock, was one of Bligh's counsel on that occasion.

Captain Bligh afterwards became a Vice-Admiral. In advancing years he found much happiness in the midst of his family, to whom he was greatly endeared. A serious internal complaint obliged him to come to London from his residence at Farningham, Kent, for surgical advice; and he died shortly afterwards in Bond Street, on the 12th of December, 1817, at the age of sixty-three.

* Dated, May 25, 1805. † Dated, December 31, 1807.

CHAPTER II.

LEGAL PROCEEDINGS IN CONSEQUENCE OF THE MUTINY—CHURCHILL AND THOMPSON—WRECK OF THE PANDORA—PETER HEYWOOD AND HIS FAMILY—LETTERS FROM NESSY HEYWOOD AND OTHERS—TRIAL OF THE MUTINEERS—THE KING'S PARDON—HONOURABLE CAREER OF CAPTAIN HEYWOOD—HIS DEATH—LINES BY ONE OF HIS CREW.

LIEUTENANT BLIGH, on his return to England in 1790, published an interesting narrative of the mutiny, and the hardships which he had endured until his landing at Timor. This excited much sympathy in his favour, and no little indignation against the mutineers.

As soon as the English government were made acquainted with the atrocious act of mutiny and piracy, of which Christian and his party had been guilty, they sent out the *Pandora* frigate, under Captain Edward Edwards, with orders to visit the Society and Friendly Islands, and use every endeavour to seize and bring home the offenders. On the arrival of that officer at Matavai Bay, off Otaheite, on the 23d of March

1791, just eighteen months after the *Bounty's* last departure from the island, three of the men, who had remained there nearly two years, namely, J. Colcman, P. Heywood, and G. Stewart, came on board the *Pandora*, and surrendered themselves to the law. They were received with all the sternness of offended justice, and instantly put in irons. The captain succeeded in taking eleven others at Otaheite, who were also carefully ironed.

Two of the mutineers, Churchill and Thompson, who had landed with the rest at Otaheite, were no longer in existence. The history of these two men has a dreadful kind of interest belonging to it. Within a short period of their quitting the *Bounty*, one of them, the ship's corporal, had become a king, and both had been murdered! Marshall, in his Naval Biography, informs us, that Churchill, after residing a short time at Matavai, accepted an invitation to live with Waheeadooa, who was sovereign of Teiarraboo, when Captain Cook last visited that place. Thompson accompanied Churchill thither; but they very soon disagreed. Waheeadooa dying without children, Churchill, who had been his *toyo*, or chief friend, succeeded to his dignity and property, according to the established custom of the country. Thompson, envious of Churchill's honours, and angry at some fancied insult, took an opportunity of shooting him. The natives rose to punish the murderer of their new sovereign, and stoned Thompson to death. This wicked man had before murdered a man and a child, but had then escaped punishment, in consequence of an error as to his person. Peter Heywood had been mistaken for him, and was on the point of being destroyed with an axe, when an old chief, who knew him, interposed, and saved his life.

Captain Edwards, after many inquiries, could hear nothing of the *Bounty*, nor of the nine remaning mutineers. But he had on board fourteen prisoners, confined in a narrow space, which was called, "Pandora's Box." It was built on the after part of the quarter-deck, and was only eleven feet in length. The voyage homeward was very disastrous, the ship being wrecked on her return on a coral reef, off the coast of New Holland, on the 29th of August, 1791, and the crew compelled to navigate 1,000 miles in open boats.

Just before the *Pandora* went down, Heywood and some other prisoners were able to disengage their hands and feet from the irons with which they had been fastened; the key of the chains having been providentially dropped through the scuttle into their prison, which was, at the time, fast filling with water. The master-at-arms, who, whether by design or accident, had dropped the key, was drowned, with thirty of the ship's company, and four of the unhappy prisoners. These four, Stewart, Sumner, Skinner, and Hillbrant, sunk in their irons.

Young Heywood seized a plank, and was swimming towards a small sandy quay about three miles off, when a boat took him up, and conveyed him thither. He sent home to his dear sister Nessy, from the ship *Hector*, in which he was afterwards confined as a prisoner, in July, 1792, two clever little sketches, which are in existence, being within a circumference not larger than that of an ordinary watch-paper. The one represents the *Pandora* sinking, as he must have caught a view of her from his plank. The other depicts the survivors on the sandy quay, which was only ninety yards long by sixty yards wide; where, under the meridian, and then vertical, sun, the only shelter the prisoners had, was to bury themselves up to their neck in the burning sand. They were on this miserable spot for nineteen days. Captain Edwards had tents, made from the boat sails, erected for himself and his people. The prisoners petitioned him for an old sail, part of the wreck, which was lying useless: but it was refused. He seems to have been needlessly severe and harsh to men, who had not yet been declared guilty, and who had an undoubted right to the common offices of humanity and respect. But, alas! there are those in every age who can find no pleasure in showing kindness to the unfortunate.

The only article saved by Heywood, on his escape from the wreck, was a Common Prayer Book, which, in swimming from the *Pandora*, he held between his teeth. It is a small edition of the year 1770.

Peter Heywood, son of Peter John Heywood, Esq., and grandson of Mr. Heywood,

Chief Justice of the Isle of Man, was born in June 1773. He had left a happy home in the Isle of Man, in August 1787, when only fourteen years old, for his first voyage in the *Bounty*, and was but a youth of between fifteen and sixteen on the occasion of the mutiny. He had now been away from his father, mother, brothers, and sisters, for five years. About the latter end of March 1790, his mother heard with grief and consternation of the mutiny which had taken place on board the *Bounty*. Her husband had died two months previous, and had thus been spared a severe domestic trial. The dreadful intelligence which reached her was aggravated by many malignant additions to the facts. She had been cruelly informed that her son, as a ringleader of the mutiny, had gone armed into Mr. Bligh's cabin. She did not, indeed, believe the account; but though she knew her dear boy's good qualities, she feared the worst results from his having been mixed up in such a transaction.

His sister, Nessy, (Hester,) had written him a letter, dated, Isle of Man, 3d June, 1792, uncertain whether he was alive or dead, and had despatched it by "the hands of Mr. Hayward, of Hackney; the father," she says, "of the young gentleman whom you so often mentioned in your letters while you were on board the *Bounty*, and who went out as third lieutenant of the *Pandora*."

After making many pathetic allusions to her brother's probable condition, and declaring her readiness, "without hesitation, to stake her life on his innocence," she adds, "How strange does it seem to me that I am now engaged in the delightful task of writing to you. Alas! my loved brother, two years ago I never expected again to enjoy such a felicity; and even yet I am in the most painful uncertainty whether you are alive. The gracious God grant that we may be at length blessed by your return. But, alas! the *Pandora's* people have been long expected, and are not even yet arrived. Should any accident have happened, after all the miseries you have already suffered, the poor gleam of hope with which we have been lately indulged, will render our situation ten thousand times more insupportable than if time had inured us to your loss."

A letter from Peter, dated Batavia, Nov. 20, 1791, at last announced that he was alive, and on his return. His account of the painful scene on board the *Bounty* afforded them, as far as he was concerned, comparative happiness. "Happening to awake," said he, "just after daylight, and looking out of my hammock, I saw a man sitting upon the arms-chest in the main hatchway, with a drawn cutlass in his hand." Being confused with the scene presented on deck, and having heard two different accounts of the object and intent of the chief actors in this deed of violence, Heywood remained awhile a silent spectator of all that was passing, until, with the best judgment which his youth and inexperience could supply on such an emergency, he decided to remain in the ship. Afterwards, on his trial, he expressed a hope, that he might be reckoned among the friends whom Bligh acknowledged he had left on board the *Bounty*. "Indeed," said Heywood, "from his attention to, and very kind treatment of me, I should have been a monster of depravity to have betrayed him."

E

Young Heywood's arrival, as a prisoner in chains, in England on the 19th of June, 1792, was in itself a relief to his distressed mother and friends. He had been conveyed from Batavia to the Cape of Good Hope in a Dutch ship, in which he had endured much hardship, and had been thence removed into the *Gorgon*, where he was treated with kindness, and allowed to walk upon deck several hours a day. Two days after his return he was transferred to the *Hector*, a 74 gun ship, commanded by Captain Montagu, which was, for upwards of eighteen weeks, his prison.

Many letters passed between Heywood and his family after his return. Mrs. Heywood, his widow, has in her possession some affecting communications from himself, his sisters, and others interested in his case. That lady, who cherishes her late husband's memory with reverence and affection, kindly placed in the hands of the author papers and letters throwing light on the severe trials, as well as on the amiable and honourable character of Mr. Heywood. She has also the Prayer Book, which he had often found a source of much comfort under his afflictions.

The present little work would evidently be incomplete without some further notice of one, who was enabled, by the good Providence of God, in whom he trusted, to live down the scandal, and heavy imputations, which, in consequence of his position and circumstances, in relation to other and older men, had fallen upon him in his youth. The following letters, which are classed according to their dates, cannot be read without emotion. Heywood was now a prisoner on board the *Hector*, at Portsmouth, awaiting his trial. He had reached Spithead, moneyless, and clad in poor apparel, which he had bought out of the produce of some straw hats made by himself, whilst his hands were in manacles.

Commodore Pasley to Mr. P. Heywood.

"SHEERNESS, *July 1st*, 1792.

"I HAVE, by this day's post, my dear young friend, written to my friend, Sir Andrew Hammond, to supply you with money, or what else you may want at present. In a day or two you shall hear from me particularly in answer to your letter. I have seen

Mr. Fryer and Cole. Rest assured of every exertion in my power to serve you. Let me hear from you, and be particular in anything in which you think I can serve you. Bear your present situation with patience and firmness. Adieu! May God grant that your innocence may be made clear, which will make happy your family and your affectionate uncle,

"THOS. PASLEY."

Heywood wrote a letter to his sisters, dated July 12, 1792, H. M. S. *Hector*, Portsmouth; beginning, "My beloved sisters all."

In this he expresses his delight at hearing from them all, and alludes to a plan which his sister Nessy had projected for a visit to him, on board the *Hector*:—"Oh, my Nessy, it grieves me to think I must be under the necessity, however heart-breaking to myself, of desiring you will relinquish your most affectionate design of coming to see me. It is too long and tedious a journey; and even on your arrival, you would not be allowed the wished-for happiness, both to you and myself, of seeing, much less conversing with your unfortunate brother. The rules of the service are so strict, that prisoners are not permitted to have any communication with female relations."

The following is an answer from his eldest sister :—

Miss Heywood to Mr. Peter Heywood.

" ISLE OF MAN, *July* 17, 1792.

" HOW can I sufficiently thank you, my dearest and most beloved boy, for your kind attention in remembering me, when I should have been the first to welcome you on your arrival in England. It is as impossible for you to conceive, as for me to express, the pleasure and satisfaction we felt on receipt of your several letters. James had your favour by the same packet which brought mine. What infinite obligations are we under, my dearest Peter, to Mr. Heywood, and his amiable daughter, Mrs. Bertie. To her kind and maternal attention you owe the re-establishment of your precious health, that blessing without which there is no real enjoyment in this life. And let it be, my dear brother, our future study to render ourselves deserving of, though it will be impossible to repay, such friendship. God grant your innocence may be, by your acquittal, speedily known to the world. I never for a moment doubted it; nor, if it was in the smallest degree suspected, would you, my dearest boy, be sustained and supported by so many friends, who, I am convinced, will do everything in their power for you. How anxiously do we all wish for the time when we shall have the inexpressible happiness of embracing you in the Isle of Man! May that period be very, very near; and may that Almighty Providence which has hitherto preserved you, watch over and protect you at the awful moment of trial. My mamma, brothers, and sisters, join in most affectionate love and ardent wishes for your safety. That you, my beloved boy, may have a speedy end to all your difficulties and distresses, and be again restored to your adoring family, is the unceasing prayer of your most sincere friend and affectionate sister,

"MARY HEYWOOD."

In the same letter, was inclosed the following from Miss Eliza Heywood:—

"How extremely happy would my beloved brother make me, if, when he has time, he would favour me with a few lines. I assure you I should be quite proud of the honour; and, as you have written to Mary, James, and Nessy, my turn must come next, or I shall feel jealous. Heaven grant we may soon embrace you in the island! You may expect to be almost suffocated with caresses for the first week. Adieu! Take care of your health, and keep up your spirits, my dear Peter. Your affectionate and faithful sister,

"ELIZA HEYWOOD."

From Nessy, in the same:—

"For me there is no room left, but to say that his faithful and affectionate Nessy sends ten thousand blessings, the best which heaven can bestow, and every wish that love and friendship can dictate to her best beloved brother, PETER."

Afterwards came the trial, and the conviction. The first clause of the 19th Article of War (22d Geo. II.) is this,—"If any person in or belonging to the fleet shall make, or endeavour to make, any mutinous assembly, on any pretence whatever; every person offending herein, and being convicted thereof, by the sentence of the court-martial shall suffer Death."

The Court-Martial for trying the prisoners was held at Portsmouth on board his Majesty's ship, *Duke*, on the 12th Sept. 1792. Bligh was absent on duty at the time. Vice-Admiral Lord Hood was the President. The officers who sat at the trial, were Captains, Sir A. S. Hamond, Bart., John Colpoys, Sir Geo. Montagu, Sir Roger Curtis, John Bazeley, Sir Andrew S. Douglas, John T. Duckworth, John N. Inglefield, John Knight, Albemarle Bertie, R. G. Keats.

The names of the ten prisoners, capitally charged with mutiny and piracy, were, Peter Heywood, James Morrison, Thomas Ellison, Thomas Burkitt, John Millward, William Musprat, Charles Norman, Joseph Coleman, Thomas M'Intosh, and Michael Byrne.

The trial was concluded on the sixth day,

the 18th of September, when the prisoners were brought in. The court having agreed, that the charges of running away with the ship, and deserting his Majesty's service, had been proved against six of the prisoners, they found Heywood, Morrison, Ellison, Burkitt, Millward, and Musprat, guilty; and adjudged them to suffer death by being hanged by the neck on board one of his Majesty's ships of war. The court acquitted the four last-mentioned prisoners, Norman, Coleman, M'Intosh, and Byrne; and recommended Peter Heywood, and James Morrison, to his Majesty's mercy.

Two days afterwards, the youthful convict wrote the following letter to the Rev. Dr. Scott, of the Isle of Man, who was a friend of the Heywood family:—

Mr. Peter Heywood to Dr. Scott.

"HECTOR, *Sept.* 20, 1792.

"HONOURED AND DEAR SIR,—On Wednesday, the 12th, the awful trial commenced, and on that day, when in court, I had the pleasure of receiving your most kind and parental letter, in answer to which I now communicate to you the melancholy issue of it, which, as I desired my friend Mr. Graham to inform you of immediately, will be no dreadful news to you. The morning lours, and all my hope of worldly joy is fled far from me. On Tuesday morning, the 18th inst., *the dreadful sentence of Death* was pronounced upon me; to which (being the just decree of that Divine Providence who first gave me breath) I bow my devoted head, with that fortitude, cheerfulness, and resignation which is the duty of every member of the Church of our blessed Saviour and Redeemer Christ Jesus. To Him alone I now look up for succour, in full hope, that perhaps a few days more will open to the view of my astonished and fearful soul His kingdom of eternal and incomprehensible bliss, prepared only for the righteous of heart. I have not been found guilty of the slightest act of the detestable crime of mutiny, but am doomed to die for not being active in my endeavour to suppress it. Could the evidences who appeared in the court-martial be tried, they would also suffer for the same and only crime of which I have been guilty. But I am to be the victim. Alas! my youthful inexperience, and no depravity of will, is the sole cause to which I can attribute my misfortunes. But so far from repining at my fate, I receive it with a dreadful kind of joy, composure, and serenity of mind, well assured that it has pleased God to point me out as a subject through whom some greatly useful, though, at present, unsearchable intention of the Divine attributes may be carried into execution for the future benefit of my country. Then why should I repine at being made a sacrifice for the good of perhaps thousands of my fellow-creatures? Forbid it, heaven! Why should I be sorry to leave a world in which I have met with nothing but misfortunes and all their concomitant evils?

"I will, on the contrary, endeavour to divest myself of all wishes for the futile and sublunary enjoyments of it, and prepare my soul for its reception into the bosom of its Redeemer. For though the very strong recommendation I have had to his Majesty's mercy by all the members of the court *may* meet with his approbation, yet that is but the balance of a straw, a mere uncertainty upon which no hope can be built. The other is a certainty which must one day happen to every mortal. Therefore the salvation of my soul requires my most powerful exertions during the short time I may have to remain on earth.

"As this is too tender a subject for me to inform my unhappy and distressed mother and sisters of, I trust, dear sir, you will either show them this letter, or make known to them the truly dreadful intelligence, in such a manner as, assisted by your wholesome and paternal advice, may enable them to bear it with Christian fortitude. The only worldly feelings I am now possessed of, are for their happiness and welfare. But even these, in my present situation, I must endeavour, with God's assistance, to eradicate from my heart, how hard soever the task. I must strive against cherishing any temporal affections. But, dear sir, endeavour to mitigate my distressed mother's sorrow. Give my everlasting duty to her, and unabated love to my disconsolate brothers and sisters, and all their relations. I have encouraged them, by my example, to bear up with fortitude and resignation to the divine will, under their load of misfortunes, almost too great for female nature to support. And teach them to be fully persuaded that all hopes of happiness on earth are vain. On my own account I still enjoy the most easy serenity of mind, and am, dearest sir, your greatly indebted and most dutiful, but ill-fated,

"PETER HEYWOOD."

It was natural for a young man, whose spirit had been well-nigh broken by sorrows of different kinds, to view his case on the dark side. Many circumstances had, indeed, come out in his favour. Bligh, when writing to Colonel Holwell, an uncle of Peter's, said, "His conduct had always given me much pleasure and satisfaction." But then it had been alleged at the trial, that he had assisted in hoisting out the launch; that he had been seen by the carpenter, resting his hand on a cutlass; and that he had laughed, on being called to by Bligh. His comments on these charges were forwarded by him to Lord Chatham, who then presided at the Admiralty. The explanations are very satisfactory, having the air of truth throughout. But he knew the unfavourable construction that might be put on doubtful acts; and he was aware that he had been neutral on an occasion of trial and danger.

Besides this, as a thoughtful person, he could not but be alive to the danger of his position, from the peculiar features of the offence of which he had been convicted. The year 1792 is memorable for the active exertions of revolutionists, and disaffected men in this country, on the one hand, and for the associations of zealous friends of the British constitution on the other. It was the avowed object of the latter to counteract all seditious proceedings, and to bring to punishment persons concerned in them. The authority of the lawful magistrate, and the claims of the established government, were to be respected and supported. The example of France, while it excited some eager spirits in the British empire to a love of change and insurrection, animated others to more energetic efforts for the maintenance of order. In the city of Paris, shortly before the execution of Louis the Sixteenth, Royalty had been declared to be abolished for ever; and it happened, that the 20th of September, 1792, the very day on which poor Heywood wrote the above admirable letter, was styled the first day of the French republic. The state of the times, therefore, tended to mark the crime imputed to him with a yet deeper dye.

Nor could the sufferer be ignorant of some then recent cases, short of murder, in which, amidst extenuating circumstances, and consequent appeals to mercy, the law had been allowed to run its course, and the capital sentence to pass into full effect.

His amiable sister Nessy, anxious to see him, and to be of use, resolved to accept the invitation given by a friend of her family, Mr. A. Graham, and to make her way up to London, where he resided. This gentleman had been a purser in the navy, and was afterwards a valuable police magistrate in London. On the 3d of October, 1792, we find Nessy arrived at Liverpool from the Isle of Man, and writing thus to her mother and family:—

"We did not arrive here till noon this

day, after a most tempestuous passage of forty-nine hours, with the wind directly contrary the whole way. Yet notwithstanding that vexatious circumstance, hard boards, aching bones in consequence, together with passing two nights almost without closing my eyes,—let me but be blessed with the cheering influence of Hope, and I have spirit to undertake anything. The plaid was a most comfortable thing to me; I wrapped it round my head. At the mouth of the river this morning, we met a small open fishing-boat, into which I got, as I was told I should, by that means, arrive two hours sooner than I should otherwise have done; and, as the sea was very high, every wave washed over me, and I had a complete wetting. On my arrival, I found poor Henry had sailed two days ago. I regret I did not come in time to see him, but I rejoice to find he went off in good spirits; and his last words mentioned *Peter!* I have been myself to secure a place in the mail-coach, and hope to be by ten o'clock to-night on my road to (may I not hope?) the completion of all my earthly happiness. Mr. Southcote, whom I passed at sea, will inform you, that the pardon went down to the King at Weymouth, some days ago. May we not, then, encourage a hope that I shall find all our misfortunes at an end? When I was tempted to repine at the winds, I remembered that they were favourable for Henry; I reflected on Peter's sufferings, and was content. Adieu, my dearest mamma, and sisters! God bless you all! In your prayers for our beloved and exemplary sufferer, add a word or two for your most dutiful and affectionate,

"NESSY HEYWOOD."

On the same day she wrote to Mr. Graham on the subject which was nearest to her heart, and which had determined her to visit London; and in a letter to her mother, dated the 5th October, Great Russell Street, the hospitable residence at which she had arrived, she announced her personal introduction to Mr. Graham, and added:—

"Well, my dear Mamma, I have had a long conversation with Mr. Graham; and, to my utmost satisfaction, he says, 'I look upon

F

him,' speaking of Peter, 'to be the most amiable young man that can possibly exist. I do not scruple to say, that I should not entirely believe you, as you may be partial; but I speak from my own observation. He conducts himself in such a manner as will reflect the highest and most lasting honour on himself, and produce the strongest sensations of pleasure and satisfaction to his friends.' Mr. Graham assures me, that there is not a doubt existing in the mind of any person who has seen the minutes of the Court-Martial, respecting Peter's innocence."

Mr. P. Heywood to Miss Nessy Heywood.

"HECTOR, *October* 16*th*, 1792.

"I have this moment, by my brother James, my beloved sister's letter of yesterday, which gives me new pleasure, from the sentiments I find my dear mother, even now, entertains of me; notwithstanding the laws of my country have condemned me to be banished from this world, as a wretch unworthy to live in it. But what of that? Am

I the first unhappy victim who has been torn from his dear family, his connexions, and his all, though conscious of his own integrity and thorough innocence of the crime for which his life must be the unjust forfeit? No! Why then should I for a moment repine? I do not, nor ever will! For that idea alone, if placed on a good foundation, is sufficient to make any man so light that he can buoyantly float upon the ruffled tide of misfortune. And I own to you, my dearest sister, it is that only which now enables me to support my life and spirits, which, without it, would soon bend beneath the ponderous load under which I have long tottered. But by and by, I shall, with God's assistance, throw it off; then all will be well, and then shall I be a joyful partaker of that bliss of which I can now have but a very faint idea! Cheer up, then, my dear Nessy! Cherish your hope, and I will exercise my patience; both, I know by experience to be productive of the same fruits of present content. James is gone to dine with Mr. Spranger, and I am employing my leisure hours in making a vocabulary of the Otaheitan language. Whomsoever you write to at home, my love, remember me to them as I wish, and in particular, to our paternal friend, Mr. Graham.

"Ever, my dearest sister, your most ardently affectionate, and truly faithful brother,

"PETER HEYWOOD.

"Keep up your dear spirits above all things. Hope is yours, and mine too."

Mr. James Heywood to Miss Nessy Heywood.

"HECTOR, 17*th October*, 1792.

"MY DEAR NESSY,—While I write this, Peter is sitting by me, making an Otaheitan vocabulary, and so happy and intent upon it, that I have no opportunity of saying a word to him. He thinks, however, you must be very busy too, or you would not deprive us of the pleasure of paying fourpence every morning. You understand me. This is the second day you have omitted it. I assure you he is at present in excellent spirits; I am perfectly convinced they are better and better every day. Don't, my dear little Ness, suppose I tell you this merely to ease your mind. No, far from it;

you must be certain I am in earnest, else I would not write in so light a strain. Adieu, dear sister. Best compliments to Mr. and Miss Graham, and believe me ever affectionately yours,

"JAMES HEYWOOD."

We know how the recommendation to mercy prevailed. King George the Third was then enjoying a visit at Weymouth, with the Queen, and the royal family. It appears from the public records of that date, that he found pleasure in doing acts of kindness; and doubtless this exercise of the royal prerogative was a cause of much inward satisfaction to the King.

On the 24th of October, 1792, the royal warrant was despatched, granting a free pardon to Heywood and Morrison, with a respite for Musprat, which was followed by a pardon; and for executing Ellison, Burkitt, and Millward.

Millward, and Musprat, with Churchill, were the men who had been deserters at Otaheite, and who had been forgiven by Bligh for that offence.

Morrison, before his connexion with the *Bounty*, had served in the navy as a midshipman; and, after his pardon, had been appointed gunner of the *Blenheim*, in which he perished with Admiral Sir Thomas Troubridge. In a violent gale on the 1st of February, 1807, that vessel was lost, with all the passengers and crew, in her way from Madras to the Cape of Good Hope.

Ellison, Burkitt, and Millward, were executed, pursuant to their sentence, on the 29th of October, on board the ship, *Brunswick*, in Portsmouth Harbour. Captain Hamond reported, that the criminals had behaved with great penitence and decorum, had acknowledged the justice of their sentence, and exhorted their fellow-sailors to take warning by their untimely fate; enjoining them, whatever might be their hardships, never to forget their obedience to their officers, but to remember the duty which they owed to their king and country. The Captain said, that a party from each ship in the harbour, and at Spithead, had attended the execution; and that, from the accounts he had received, the example seemed to have made a salutary impression on the minds of all the ships' companies present.

The following words were used by Mr. Heywood, when Captain Montague had read to him his Majesty's free and unconditional pardon, on the 27th of October;

"SIR, When the sentence of the law was passed upon me, I received it, I trust, as became a man; and if it had been carried into execution, I should have met my fate, I hope, in a manner becoming a Christian. Your admonition cannot fail to make a lasting impression upon my mind. I receive with gratitude my sovereign's mercy, for which my future life shall be faithfully devoted to his service."

The pardon was a source of unspeakable delight to his family, especially to his sister Nessy, whose peace of mind had been broken by the terror of losing him by an ignominious death, and whose joy, on hearing of his pardon was, perhaps, more difficult to bear than her previous grief had been:

"For sudden joys, like griefs, confound at first."

She had written to her mother and sisters

on the 26th, inclosing a statement of the pardon having been transmitted to Portsmouth. In this letter she said, "O blessed hour! Little did I think, my beloved friends, when I closed my letter this morning, that before night I should be out of my senses with joy. This moment, this ecstatic moment, brought the inclosed. I cannot speak my happiness. I am too *mad* to write sense; but 'tis a pleasure I would not forego to be the most reasonable being on earth."

In this way the family received the delightful intelligence; and the warm-hearted and untiring Mr. Graham, unable to remain easy at home, hastened to Portsmouth to congratulate his young friend, and bring him to London. Nothing can be more hearty or natural than the following:—

A. Graham, Esq. to Miss N. Heywood.

"PORTSMOUTH, *Oct. 27th,* 1792.

"MY DEAREST NESSY,

"If you expect me to enter into particulars as to *how* I got him, *when* I got him, and *where* I have him, you will be disappointed; for that is not in my power at present.

Suffice it to say that he is now with me, and well; *not on board the* HECTOR, but at the house of a very worthy man. To-day we dine with Mr. Delafons; to-morrow we shall, perhaps, sleep on the London road; and on Tuesday,—Oh, my dear little girl! Kiss Maria for me, and tell her I love her dearly, and am,

"Yours most affectionately,

"A. GRAHAM."

To this letter the following postscript was added:—

From Peter Heywood to Nessy.

"P.S. Be patient, my dearest Nessy. A few hours, and you will embrace your long-lost and most affectionate brother,

"PETER HEYWOOD."

Mr. Graham's impatience, and generous anxiety to crown this joyful event, would not permit him to delay one moment; and on the Monday morning, the happy party arrived in London.

On the 29th October a letter was written, apprising the anxious mother of her dear sailor boy's arrival in London. Another letter, written after poor Nessy had seen him at liberty, breathes the tenderest feelings of a heart almost breaking with joy. It is thus headed:

"Great Russell-street. Monday morning, 29th Oct., half-past ten o'clock, the brightest moment of my existence," and ends thus:—

"I can write no more, but to tell you, that the three happiest beings at this moment on earth are your most dutiful and affectionate children, NESSY HEYWOOD, PETER HEYWOOD, JAMES HEYWOOD."

This amiable girl possessed, among other accomplishments, poetic powers of no common order. There remain in manuscript many copies of verses of her composition on various subjects; though her theme of themes was her brother, his sufferings, and his restoration to liberty and honour. The following are among the lines which she wrote, "*On receiving certain intelligence that my most amiable and beloved brother, Peter Heywood, would soon be restored to freedom:*"—

O, blissful hour!—O moment of delight!
Replete with happiness, with rapture bright.
An age of pain is sure repaid by this;
'Tis joy too great—'tis ecstacy of bliss.

My beating heart, oppress'd with woe and care,
Has yet to learn such happiness to bear.
From grief, distracting grief, thus high to soar,
To know dull pain and misery no more,
To hail each op'ning morn with new delight,
To rest in peace and joy each happy night,
To see my Lycidas from bondage free,
Restored to life, to pleasure, and to me;
To see him thus, adorn'd with virtue's charms,
To give him to a longing mother's arms,
To know him by surrounding friends caress'd;
Of honour, fame, of life's best gifts possess'd;
Oh, my full heart! 'tis joy, 'tis bliss supreme,
And though 'tis real,—yet, how like a dream!
Then teach me, Heav'n, to bear it as I ought;
Inspire each rapt'rous, each transporting thought
Teach me to bend beneath thy bounteous hand,
With gratitude my willing heart expand:
To Thy Omnipotence I humbly bow,
Afflicted once—but ah! how happy now!

What reader does not wish to learn more about Nessy Heywood? In less than a year after her beloved brother's liberation, whilst still in her youthful days, she was called away from taking a part in this busy anxious world. It no longer remained for her to "rejoice with them that do rejoice, and weep with them that weep." Active and alert no more in the service of those she loved, she was to seek her employment and consolation in her sick chamber; and there is reason to believe, that, trusting in her Redeemer's merits, she found comfort in true Religion, without which the ties of affection must, she knew, be utterly dissolved, the enjoyment derived from it pass away for ever.

In the manuscript collection, from which the above letters and verses have been extracted, is a memorandum by Mrs. Heywood, (Peter's mother,) in her own handwriting, dated, Douglas, Isle of Man, shortly after Nessy's death. "My dearest Nessy was seized, while on a visit at Major Yorke's, at Bishop's Grove, near Tunbridge Wells, with a violent cold; and, not taking proper care of herself, it soon turned to inflammation on her lungs, which carried her off at Hastings, to which place she was taken on the 5th of September, to try if the change of air, and being near the sea, would recover her. But, alas! it was too late for her to receive the wished-for benefit, and she died there on the 25th of the same month, 1793, and has left her only surviving parent a disconsolate mother, to lament, while ever she lives, with the most sincere affliction, the irreparable loss of her most valuable, affectionate, darling daughter."

Having, on his release, visited his family and friends, Mr. Heywood, as soon as his health was completely restored, re-entered the navy, by the desire of Captain Pasley, (afterwards Sir Thomas Pasley, Bart.) and on the express recommendation of Lord Hood, who had presided at his court-martial. Indeed, Lord Hood offered to take him under his own immediate patronage; but this was declined with thanks by Captain Pasley, who, on the 17th May, 1793, received him under his own command, into the *Bellerophon*.

In consideration of the King's free pardon, it was decided that no incapacity existed for his thus again fully undertaking the duties of his profession. In January 1797, after he had done his duty in several actions with the French fleet, Earl Spencer, who had attentively considered the several points connected with the court-martial of 1792, wrote to Sir Thomas Pasley, to say that those circumstances ought not to be allowed to stand in the way of Mr. Heywood's further progress in his profession; "more especially," said his lordship, "when the gallantry and propriety of his conduct, in his subsequent service, are taken into consideration. I shall therefore have no difficulty in mentioning him to the commander-in-chief on the station to which he belongs, as a person from whose promotion, on a proper opportunity, I shall derive much satisfaction."

He became a post-captain in 1803, and after a career of important and responsible service, including two diplomatic missions to South America, he was, on the 29th July, 1813, appointed to the command of the *Montagu*, of 74 guns, in which he served in the North Sea, and afterwards in the Mediterranean, under the command of Lord Exmouth.

On Captain Heywood's return, the *Montagu* was paid off at Chatham, on the 16th July, 1816; and he came ashore, after having been actively employed at sea twenty-seven years, six months, one week, and five days, out of a service in the navy of twenty-nine years, seven months, and one day.

On the 18th May, 1818, Lord Melville, without any solicitation, made him the offer of the command, with a Commodore's broad pendant, on the lakes in Canada. A considerable salary was annexed to this important office; but as he had married in 1816, and there was no war requiring his active exertions for the benefit of his country, Captain Heywood, with Lord Melville's permission, declined the proffered honour; and he afterward found his chief happiness in the bosom of his family. His career of activity being now at an end in an honourable profession, which had acknowledged and appreciated a life of useful labour, his early afflictions, the sufferings of body and soul, began to tell upon his constitution. It is thought, that during the period of his imprisonment, the seeds were sown of that disorder, (a complaint of the heart,) which terminated his existence. Bligh, in his account of the mutineers, which was drawn up at Timor, in 1789, says, after describing Heywood's height and person; "At this time he has not done growing."

Whilst his body was ripening into manhood, the iron entered into his soul.

This valuable and excellent officer died in London on the 10th February, 1831, in his fifty-eighth year, and was buried in a vault at Highgate Chapel.

There is not room in these pages for an enumeration of his professional services; but Lieut. Marshall, in his Naval Biography, supplies the deficiency by the following passage, written in 1825, respecting him:—

"The misfortunes of his youth proved highly beneficial to him. The greater part of those distinguished officers who had sat as members of the court-martial, justly considering him much more unfortunate than criminal, extended their patronage to him immediately after his release; and through their good offices, and his own meritorious behaviour, he was subsequently advanced, step by step, to the rank he at present holds. The duties which have fallen to his share he has ever performed with a zeal not inferior to that of any other officer in the service. The young men who have had the honour of serving under him, many of whom now enjoy commissions, will readily and gratefully acknowledge, that, both by precept, and his own example, he invariably endeavoured to form their characters, as men and officers, in the solid principles of religion and virtue. In short, we do not hesitate to say, that his king and country never had a more faithful servant, nor the naval service a more worthy and respectable member."

What a chequered and eventful life was his! How zealously must he have laboured in his profession, who could have earned, at the age of forty-three, such ample testimonies to his merit. This chapter cannot conclude better than with a spirited stanza from a copy of verses, written by one of the *Montagu's* crew, and sent to Captain Heywood, by desire of the whole ship's company, when that vessel was put out of commission in 1816:—

"Farewell to thee, HEYWOOD! a truer one never
Hath exercised rule o'er the sons of the wave;
The seamen who served thee would serve *thee* for ever,
Who sway'd, but ne'er fetter'd, the hearts of the brave."

G

CHAPTER III

CHRISTIAN AND HIS PARTY—PITCAIRN'S ISLAND—FOLGER'S ACCOUNT—LANDING OF NINE MUTINEERS AND OTHERS AT PITCAIRN—DREADFUL DEATHS OF CHRISTIAN AND OTHERS—INTOLERABLE STATE OF SOCIETY AT PITCAIRN —INTEMPERANCE—REPENTANCE AND REFORMATION OF ADAMS—HIS SERVICES IN THE CAUSE OF RELIGION AND MORALITY IN THE ISLAND.

NOTHING more was heard of Christian and his party, until twenty years had passed from the date of the mutiny; when Sir Sidney Smith, then commander-in-chief on the Brazil station, informed the Admiralty, from Rio Janciro, that Captain Folger, of the ship *Topaz*, of Boston, United States, on landing on Pitcairn's Island, in 1808, had found an Englishman, named Alexander Smith, the only person remaining of nine that had found their way thither in the *Bounty*. Smith, otherwise John Adams, (who had, on first entering the service, assumed the name of Alexander Smith,) related, that after putting Bligh into the boat, Christian, with the other mutineers, had gone to Otaheite, where all hands remained, but Christian, Smith, and seven others; that each had taken an Otaheitan wife, and then proceeded to Pitcairn, where they had made good a landing, and afterwards broken up the *Bounty*.

This brings our readers to Pitcairn's Island. Some of them may desire to learn the origin of its name, and the circumstances of its first discovery by British navigators.

Captain Philip Carteret, in his description of a Voyage round the World, wrote as follows, July 1767 :—

"We continued our course westward till the evening of Thursday, the 2d of July, when we discovered land to the northward of us. Upon approaching it the next day, it appeared like a great rock rising out of the sea. It was not more than five miles in circumference, and seemed to be uninhabited. It was, however, covered with trees; and we saw a small stream of fresh water running down one side of it. I would have landed upon it, but the surf, which at this season broke upon it with great violence, rendered it impossible. I got soundings on the west side of it, at somewhat less than a mile from the shore, in twenty-five fathoms, with a bottom of coral and sand; and it is probable that in fine summer weather landing here may not only be practicable, but easy. We saw a great number of sea-birds hovering about it, at somewhat less than a mile from the shore; and the sea here seemed to have fish. It lies in lat. 20° 2′ south: long. 133° 21′ west. It is so high, that we saw it at the distance of more than fifteen leagues; and it having been discovered by a young gentleman, son to Major Pitcairn, of the marines, we called it PITCAIRN'S ISLAND. This young man was unfortunately lost in the *Aurora*.*

"While we were in the neighbourhood of this island, the weather was extremely tempestuous, with long rolling billows from the southward, larger and higher than any I had

* His father, Major Pitcairn, was killed at the battle of Bunker's Hill, in America, in 1775.

seen before. The winds were variable, but blew chiefly from the SS.W., W. and W.N.W. We had very seldom a gale to the eastward; so that we were prevented from keeping in a high south latitude, and were constantly driving to the northward."*

Pitcairn's Island, distant about 1,200 miles from Otaheite, is of volcanic origin. The peculiar features of the volcanic islands, of which there are several in the South Seas, show that they have been elevated from the bed of the ocean by the resistless force of fire, which has given a vertical character, and jagged outline, to their rocky mountains, and greatly increased the wild beauties of their scenery. Pitcairn is in latitude 25° 4′ south, and longitude 130° 8′ west; and the highest point is about 1,008 feet above the level of the sea. In clear weather the island may be seen at forty miles' distance. It is four miles and a half in circumference, one mile and a half being the

* Voyage round the World, by Captain P. Carteret, Commander of H. M. Sloop, *Swallow*, in 1766-7-8-9. Passage from Mas-afuera to Queen Charlotte's Islands. Chap. iii.

greatest length. The climate, which is just without the tropics, is adapted for the production of useful vegetables, which form the chief article of food:—Irish and sweet potatoes, yams, bread-fruit, a vegetable called taro (*Arum esculentum*), pumpkins, Indian maize, and beans. Here and there are patches of the tobacco-plant, and sugar-canes. The fruits are pines, plantains, and bananas, oranges, limes, melons, a species of apple, and cocoa-nuts. Among the trees are the Cocoa-nut (*Cocos nucifera*); the Plantain (*Musa paradisiaca*); the Bread-fruit tree (*Artocarpus incisa*); the Nono (*Morinda citrifolia*), &c.; but the most striking and remarkable is the Banyan (*Ficus Indica*):—

> "The fig-tree; not that kind for fruit renown'd,
> But such as at this day to India known,
> In Malabar or Deccan spreads her arms,
> Branching so broad and long, that in the ground
> The bended twig takes root, and daughters grow
> About the mother-tree, a pillar'd shade,
> High over-reach'd, and echoing walks between.
> There oft the Indian herdsman, shunning heat,
> Shelters in cool, and tends his pasturing herds
> At loop-holes cut through thickest shade."
>
> MILTON.

The temperature of Pitcairn ranges from

'LOOK-OUT RIDGE,' AND CHRISTIAN'S HOUSE, PITCAIRN.

59° in winter to 87° in summer. The average is 65° in winter, and 82° in summer. The vegetation sometimes suffers from swarms of insects. To remedy this evil, there having been on the island only one species of land bird, a small fly-catcher, it was thought desirable to convey some birds to the spot. Her Majesty's Ship, *Virago*, Commander Prevost, left Callao for Pitcairn, in January 1853, having on board singing-birds, rose-trees, myrtles, &c. for the islanders.

There are lizards, but no venomous reptiles on the island. The people are annoyed by rats; which do much damage to the sugar-canes. Hence the strictness of the law for the preservation of cats.*

About half the island, consisting of six hundred acres, is cultivated. The rest is considered too rocky for cultivation. There being but little beach, the quantity of sea-weed washed up is small; such as there is, however, is employed for the use of the ground.

Though the climate cannot be called unhealthy, the people are not generally long-

* See page 245.

lived. Arthur Quintal, the oldest man among them, is only fifty-seven; Elizabeth Young, daughter of the late John Mills, though the oldest person on the island, is but sixty. The ailments to which the islanders are most subject are, rheumatism, influenza, bilious affections, and diseases of the heart.

Nature has fortified the coast with powerful barriers, which render it most difficult of access, except in Bounty Bay, situate on the north-east side; and even there the approach is impossible when the sea is high. The ships, which occasionally remain awhile in the neighbourhood of the island, and for which there is abundance of water, stand off and on as well as they may, and as the wind allows them. Though soundings in from 25 to 35 fathoms may be obtained at some distance, anchorage is seldom resorted to; the state of the ground being such as to cause a risk of losing the anchor. Lofty bristling rocks, one of which is called St. Paul's Point, rise perpendicularly from the sea; and cliffs, with clumps of cocoa-nut-trees at their base, are seen, as the boats approach the beach, which is shingly, and very narrow at the place of landing. The landing is effected in the boats of the natives; these being better suited than ships' boats for passing the breakers.

"Having set foot on shore," says Mr. Brodie, who was there in March 1850, "you ascend a steep hill, almost a cliff, for about three hundred yards, to a table-land, planted with cocoa-nut-trees, which is called the market-place, about a quarter of a mile beyond which, at the north end of the island, lies the settlement, flanked by a grove of cocoa-nut-trees, kumeras, and plantains, &c. which make the approach very picturesque."*

Though the island, according to Captain Carteret, owes its name to young Mr. Pitcairn, he having been the first native of this kingdom who noted the place, it was doubtless once known by some other name, which is now lost, together with all traces of its former inhabitants, except a few human skeletons, idols, and weapons, which were discovered there by the mutineers. It has become a clear matter of fact, that the

* "Pitcairn's Island, and the Islanders in 1850." By Walter Brodie.

island was inhabited previously to their arrival. Overlooking Bounty Bay is a lofty peak, within 100 yards of which were found on a rock four images, about six feet in height, placed upon a platform, which is called a *paipai.* One of these was a rude representation of the human figure, to the hips, hewn out of a piece of red lava. Each of the skulls which were dug up had under it a pearl-shell, according to the mode of burial adopted in the place at the time, probably some centuries since. It has been suggested with reason, that the ancient occupants were drifted to this place from the Gambier, or other islands, on a raft. Several specimens of hatchets, and spear-heads of very hard stone, and a large stone bowl, were discovered. The mutineers also met, on the east side of the island, with certain uncouth carvings of the sun, moon, stars, a bird, men, &c. in a cavern situate in the face of a cliff.

There are some inaccuracies in the narrative forwarded by Captain Folger, in his letter of March 1, 1813, respecting his visit to the island. He stated that about six years after the arrival of the nine mutineers, the

Otaheitans had killed all the Englishmen, except Smith, who was severely wounded; and that on the same night the Otaheitan widows had risen, and murdered all their countrymen, leaving only Smith, with the widows and children. His account may be corrected by the following statement:—

After getting rid of Mr. Bligh, and his crew, the mutineers sailed for Toubouai, an island about 500 miles south of Otaheite, where they intended to land; but the natives refusing to admit them, they proceeded to Otaheite. A second ineffectual attempt at settling having been made on Toubouai, and a refuge having again been found, for a short time, at Otaheite, Christian and eight of his comrades left for Pitcairn, in the *Bounty*, with certain Otaheitans, the rest of the mutineers remaining at Otaheite. It happened that Carteret's description of Pitcairn had been on board the *Bounty;* and this probably determined Christian in his choice. Carteret, however, as will have been seen, was wrong in his statement of the latitude and longitude of the island.

When the *Bounty* arrived at Pitcairn's

Island, she had on board nine Englishmen, with nine Otaheitan women, their wives; six Otaheitan men, three of whom had wives; and a little girl; making twenty-eight persons who landed. This little girl, then an infant of ten months old, was afterwards the wife of Charles Christian, and the mother of Mr. G. H. Nobbs's wife. The names of the nine mutineers who reached the Island in the *Bounty* were—

FLETCHER CHRISTIAN . . .	Master's Mate.
EDWARD YOUNG	Midshipman.
JOHN MILLS	Gunner's Mate.
MATTHEW QUINTAL	Seaman.
WILLIAM M'COY	Ditto.
ALEXANDER SMITH, alias JOHN ADAMS	Ditto
JOHN WILLIAMS	Ditto
ISAAC MARTIN	Ditto
WILLIAM BROWN	Gardener.

Christian and Young were men of good education. The former was the brother of Edward Christian, Esq. Professor of Law at Cambridge, Chief Justice of Ely, and Editor of Blackstone's Commentaries. Young was a nephew of Sir George Young, Bart. The other mutineers who landed at Pitcairn were chiefly sailors of the ordinary class.

They had not long set foot upon the island when it became a stage for the display of every evil passion. They were "hateful, and hating one another." During the frightful period of domestic warfare between the Europeans and the blacks, in which the former often adopted the tremendously simple rule of might against right, the blacks made common cause together, and planned the murder of their imperious masters. This plot reached the ears of the wives of the mutineers: and the females are said to have disclosed it to their husbands, just before the time appointed for the massacre, by adding to one of their songs these words, "Why does black man sharpen axe? To kill white man." In the course of the deadly struggles occurring between the several parties, Christian, Mills, Williams, Martin, and Brown, were murdered in the year 1793 by the Otaheitan men whom they had brought to the island with them. All the Otaheitan men were killed in the same year, one of them having been destroyed by Young's wife with an axe. As soon as she had killed the last survivor but one of the Otaheitans, she gave a signal to her husband to fire upon the remaining black, which was done with fatal precision. This woman, Susannah, who afterwards married Thursday October Christian, Fletcher Christian's son, died at an advanced age in the year 1850. She was the last survivor of the *Bounty*.

The sanguinary frays among the members of the small body of inhabitants, from the time of their landing, to 1794, have been described at different times. These painful particulars shall be passed over. One point, however, connected with the murders deserves mention, as it may serve to clear up some doubt regarding the death of Fletcher Christian. As the spot in which he was buried on the island is not known, and as a person resembling him was seen, about the year 1809, in Fore Street, Plymouth, by Captain Peter Heywood, who imagined, from a transient view, that the stranger was Fletcher Christian himself, an impression in some quarters prevailed, that he had escaped the massacre of 1793, and had returned to England. But the manuscript documents of the island seemed to be clear upon this matter. In 1794, when only four men,

Young, M'Coy, Adams, and Quintal, were left alive, the women of the place were seen with the *five skulls* of the murdered white men, and were compelled, after some difficulty, to give them up to be buried.

In that year the state of the island had become so intolerable to the women, that they resolved to brave the perils of the sea, rather than remain. They had accordingly prepared to set off secretly in a boat, which, fortunately for them, upset in launching; as the men who had built it probably intended it should do; and the women, foiled in their attempt to get away, again settled down in their sad and unwelcome home. Whither they had proposed to go, it is impossible to say. The nearest island to Pitcairn, nearly ninety miles to its north, is Oeno, of coral formation, a barren place, most difficult of access. The approach is so bad, owing to the reefs of coral encompassing the lagoon which surrounds the island, that when Captain Beechey, in December 1825, attempted to land, the boat was broken to pieces. Lieut. Edward Belcher narrowly escaped with his life, and a young lad of the party was drowned.

There is also, about 120 miles from Pitcairn, Elizabeth, or Henderson's Island, so called after Captain Henderson, of the *Hercules*, of Calcutta. It is nearly eighty feet above the level of the sea, five miles in length, one mile in breadth, of volcanic formation, and covered with dead coral. The soil is poor and sandy. There are many trees and shrubs on the island, and it has been occasionally visited by the Pitcairn people, chiefly for the sake of the timber found there. On the occasion of their visit in 1851, they found eight human skeletons lying in caves; probably the remains of some shipwrecked mariners, who, unable to procure food or water, had lain down to die.

The women, in the same year in which they had endeavoured to quit Pitcairn, deliberately planned the destruction of the four men left among them. This dreadful plot was discovered in time by the men; and a partial and suspicious peace was brought about.

But other horrors remained behind. In 1798, M'Coy, in a fit of *delirium tremens*, brought on by drunkenness, having thrown himself from the rocks into the sea, was

CORAL ISLAND.

drowned. Quintal, a violent and headstrong man, after threatening the lives of his companions, was killed by Young and Adams, who, in 1799, took away his life with an axe in self-defence. Thus, six of the mutineers were murdered, and one committed suicide. Edward Young died of asthma, in 1800. Adams had been severely wounded in one of the contests that took place, but had recovered. Only two of the fifteen men, who had landed from the *Bounty* (Young and Adams) died a natural death.

Here we may pause to reflect on the unhappy lives and dreadful deaths of men who had been guilty of a very heinous offence against the laws of God and man. Though Christian, when fixed at Pitcairn, often wore a cheerful countenance and manner, there is reason to believe that the remembrance of the past was deeply painful to him, and that shame and remorse, mingled with the fear of detection, weighed heavily on his mind.

On the top of a high rock, is a spot which he called his "look-out." Whilst many hearts, thousands of miles off, were wounded, if not broken, by suspense and uncertainty respecting the fate of himself and his companions, he was either employed in surveying the ocean around him, under the apprehension of the approach of the officers of justice, or in endeavouring to control the turbulent community, among whom he had irrevocably cast his lot.

It may be observed, that punishment in this life often bears a startling likeness to the sin which has been committed, and which not only thus finds the offender out, but shows him that it has done so. Within the narrow limits of the island, as in the confines of a ship, Christian had enemies at hand, who harassed, and at length took away his life; and it is a remarkable fact, that he who had raised his hand in a criminal manner against his superior in command, should have suffered death from those whom he looked upon as under his authority.

Nor must it be forgotten, that one chief cause of all the quarrels and miseries of the mutineers, was intemperance. M'Coy had unhappily become acquainted with the art of distilling; and, with the aid of a copper boiler, which had been taken from the *Bounty*, and which was altered into a still, he soon made ardent spirit out of the ti-root (*Dracæna terminalis*). This served to thin yet further the number of the original male settlers, until only one of them was left remaining.

It pleased God to touch the heart of that one, and to make him an instrument of good to those around him. His deceased comrades had left families, who had been brought up in ignorance of their God and Saviour, all the women being Otaheitan idolaters. One Bible, and one only, which had been occasionally read by Christian and Young, remained: this inestimable treasure having been rescued from the *Bounty*. Here was a merciful provision for guiding Adams, and those around him, in the right way, and making them wise unto salvation. It may even be hoped that the blessing had not been lost upon Christian and Young.

Besides the Holy Scriptures, Adams had the comfort and advantage of possessing a Common Prayer Book, one copy of which had also been recovered from the ship: and of this he made constant use.

In the year 1800, having then reached his

thirty-sixth year, he found himself the only man on the island. The younger part, consisting of twenty children, looked up to him with reverence and affection. About ten years after this, he had two remarkable dreams, which presented to him in vivid colours his past transgressions, and the awful nature of the punishment awaiting them. These were such dreams as many persons may have had in their turns; but they produced in him a lasting and wholesome impression, and effectually moved his conscience. May we not believe this to have been the influence of the Holy Spirit, whose merciful design it was to give him a better knowledge of himself, and of the justice and goodness of God, and to bring him an humble suppliant to the throne of grace, for the pardon of his sins, through the merits of a crucified Saviour? "Behold, I stand at the door, and knock: if any man hear my voice, and open the door, I will come in to him," &c. (Rev. iii. 20.)

Let no one say that there is any encouragement to superstition in these remarks. That which is uppermost in the thoughts, though it may not have ripened into good

R. Beechey
to The Queen

resolutions, much less into right practice, is frequently displayed in a manner, strong as reality, in those solemn hours, when the world is shut out, and deep sleep falleth upon man. An idea, which has been presented to the mind whilst we are awake, often assumes, by reflection, and during the hours of sleep, a solemnity and importance which it did not before possess. And perhaps there are no inward admonitions more affecting, or more fruitful of good, than those which relate to our children, and to the obligations under which we are laid to conduct the young in the right way. Happy are they who are wise enough to make a good use of that which appears to have been sent to them for a good end. Adams had begun to read his Bible; and who can tell the power given by the grace of God to the study of the revealed Word, with prayer, and to a thoughtful and candid perusal of the injunctions of the Saviour, to whom the young were objects of the tenderest regard?

With his clearer view of the parental character, and of the condition of his own soul, Adams became a religious man. He instructed the young people about him in the fear of God. He prayed for them, and for himself. He observed the rules of the Church of England, always had morning and evening prayers, and taught the children the Collects, and other portions of the Prayer Book, beginning with the Lord's Prayer, and the Apostles' Creed. He was afterwards very fond of reading a book published by the *Society for Promoting Christian Knowledge*, entitled, "The Knowledge and Practice of Christianity; an Instruction for the Indians. By the Right Rev. Dr. Wilson, Bishop of Sodor and Man." His youthful pupils took such delight in his instructions, that, on one occasion, on his offering to two of the lads, Arthur Quintal and Robert Young, some compensation for their labour in preparing ground for planting yams, they proposed, that, instead of his giving the present held out to them, consisting of a small quantity of gunpowder, he should teach them some extra lessons out of the Bible; a request with which he joyfully complied.

Adams was no ordinary man, or he could never have accomplished the arduous task which he had undertaken to perform. By a steadfast adherence to the line of duty which he had marked out for his conduct, he could not but perceive that the blessing of God was upon his labours. The fruits of good became apparent in a place where indifference to religion, and looseness of morals had prevailed; and when we consider the latter part of his pilgrimage, and the filial reverence with which he was regarded by his juniors, we may conclude that this island-patriarch had much to cheer and encourage him, amidst the trials and sorrows which had come upon him. Among the most comfortable feelings of his heart, as the end of his existence drew on, was probably the well-grounded hope that the rising generation would fear God, and keep His commandments. Looking at the improved condition of the people, just previously to his death, which happened in March 1829, when he was sixty-five years of age, he might well have been gladdened by the prospect of the continuance among them of those firm and solid principles of true religion which had been fixed upon a sure foundation, and which form a topic of honourable mention at this very time.

Much of Adams's trouble and anxiety in former years naturally arose from the fear of being discovered and taken. In May 1795 he, and his brother-mutineers, having observed a ship nearing the island, in their terror hid themselves in the bush. Having cautiously left their place of concealment, they found a knife by the sea-side, and a few cocoa-nut shells, proving that some persons had landed. The visitors, however, it would seem, had not noticed any signs of houses, and had therefore proceeded on their voyage.

CHAPTER IV.

DESCRIPTION OF THE STATE OF PITCAIRN IN 1814, AND SUBSEQUENT YEARS—ACCOUNT GIVEN BY SIR THOMAS STAINES, AND CAPTAIN BEECHEY—EMIGRATION TO OTAHEITE IN 1831—QUEEN POMARÉ—HER LETTER TO QUEEN VICTORIA.

ON the occasion of Captain Folger's visit to Pitcairn in 1808, he had carried away a chronometer and compass, originally belonging to the *Bounty*, for the purpose of forwarding them to the Admiralty. But no further notice was taken of the island, nor of its inhabitants, until 1814, when his Majesty's ships *Briton* and *Tagus*, Captain Sir Thomas Staines, and Captain Pipon, being in search of an American ship of war, the *Essex*, which had been seizing some of our whaling vessels, arrived at Pitcairn. Adams now supposed that his time was come, and that he should be carried away. Though much alarmed, he did not attempt concealment, but presented himself to the officers, who soon reassured him by saying that he was not to be arrested; the time was past for that: he had been a quarter of a century in the island; and his presence was useful to the islanders.

The condition of the place and people at that date cannot be better described than by Sir T. Staines in his own words, in a letter addressed by him to Vice-Admiral Manley Dixon:—

"*Briton*, Valparaiso, Oct. 18th, 1814.

"SIR,—I have the honour to inform you that on my passage from the Marquesas Islands to this point, on the morning of the 17th September, I fell in with an island where none is laid down in the Admiralty or other charts, according to the several chronometers of the *Briton* and *Tagus*. I therefore hove to, until daylight, and then closed, to ascertain whether it was inhabited, which I soon discovered it to be, and, to my great astonishment, found that every individual on the island (forty in number) spoke very good English. They proved to be the descendants of the deluded crew of the *Bounty*, which from Otaheite proceeded to the abovementioned island, where the ship was burnt.

"Christian appeared to have been the leader, and the sole cause of the mutiny in that ship. A venerable old man, named John Adams, is the only surviving Englishman of those who last quitted Otaheite in her, and whose exemplary conduct, and fatherly care of the whole little colony, could not but command admiration. The pious manner in which all those born on the island have been reared, the correct sense of religion which has been instilled into their young minds by this old man, has given him the preeminence over the whole of them, to whom they look up as the father of the whole, and one family.

"A son of Christian was the first born on the island, now about twenty-five years of age (named Thursday October Christian); the elder Christian fell a sacrifice to the jealousy of an Otaheitan man, within three or four years after their arrival on the island. They were accompanied thither by six Otaheitan men and twelve women; the former were all swept away by desperate contentions between them and the Englishmen, and five of the latter have died at different periods, leaving at present only one man and several women, of the original settlers.

"The island must, undoubtedly, be that called Pitcairn, although erroneously laid down in the charts. We had the meridian sun close to it, which gave us 25 deg. 4 min. S. latitude, and 130 deg. 25 min. W. longitude, by chronometers of the *Briton* and *Tagus*. It is abundant in yams, plantains, hogs, goats, and fowls, but affords no shelter for a ship or vessel of any description: neither could a ship water there without great difficulty.

"I cannot refrain from offering my opinion, that it is well worthy the attention of our laudable religious Societies, particularly that for propagating the Christian religion, the whole of the inhabitants speaking the Otaheitan tongue as well as English. During the whole of the time they have been on the island, only one ship has ever communicated with them, which took place about six years since, by an American ship, called the *Topaz*, of Boston, Mayhew Folger, master. The island is completely iron-bound, with rocky shores, and landing in boats at all times difficult, although safe to approach within a short distance in a ship.

(Signed) "T. STAINES."

It is rather remarkable, that in this letter John Adams should have been styled a "venerable old man," as he was then only fifty years of age. But he had suffered much anxiety; for a long period of his life he had been a stranger to security; and his weather-beaten face bore marks of a more advanced age than that which he had attained. He is mentioned in Bligh's description, as very much pitted with the small-pox, and "tattowed on his body, legs, arms, and feet."

As the real position of the island was ascertained to be far distant from that in which it had been usually laid down in the charts, and as Sir T. Staines and Captain Pipon seem to have still considered it as uninhabited, they were not a little surprised, on approaching its shores, to behold plantations regularly laid out, and huts or houses, more neatly constructed than those of the Marquesas Islands. When about two miles from the landing-place, some natives were observed bringing down their canoes on their shoulders, dashing through a heavy surf, and paddling off to the ships; but the astonishment of our sailors was unbounded on hearing one of the natives, on approaching the ship, call out in the English language, "Won't you heave us a rope, now?"

The first man who got on board the *Briton* soon proved who they were. His name, he said, was Thursday October Christian, the first born on the island,* son of Fletcher Christian. He was then about twenty-five years of age, a fine young man, about six feet high, his hair deep black; his countenance open and interesting; of a brownish cast, but free from all that mixture of a reddish tint which prevails on the Pacific islands; his only dress was a piece of cloth round his loins, and a straw hat, ornamented with the black feathers of the domestic fowl. "With a great share of good humour," says Captain Pipon, "we were glad to trace in his benevolent countenance all the features of an honest English face. I must confess,"

* He was born on a Thursday in October.

he continues, "I could not survey this interesting person without feelings of tenderness and compassion. His companion was named George Young, a fine youth, of seventeen or eighteen years of age."

If the astonishment of the captains was great on hearing their first salutation in English, their surprise and interest were not a little increased, on Sir Thomas Staines taking the youths below and setting before them something to eat, when one of them rose up, and placing his hands together in a posture of devotion, distinctly repeated, and in a pleasing tone and manner, "For what we are going to receive, the Lord make us truly thankful."

They expressed great surprise on seeing a cow on board the *Briton*, and were in doubt whether she was a great goat, or a horned sow.

The two captains of his Majesty's ships accompanied these young men on shore. With some difficulty, and a good wetting, and with the assistance of their conductors, they accomplished a landing through the surf, and were soon after met by John

Adams, who conducted them to his house. His wife accompanied him, an old person, blind and infirm. He was at first alarmed, lest the visit was to apprehend him; but, on being told that they had been perfectly ignorant of his existence, he was relieved from his anxiety. Being once assured that the visit was of a peaceable nature, it is impossible to describe the joy these poor people manifested on seeing those whom they were pleased to consider as their countrymen. Yams, cocoa-nuts, and other fruits, with fine fresh eggs, were laid before them; and Adams would have killed and dressed a hog for his visitors, but time would not allow them to partake of the intended feast.

This interesting settlement then consisted of about forty-six persons, mostly grown up young people, besides a number of infants. The young men, all born on the island, were very athletic, and of fine forms, their countenances open and pleasing, indicating much benevolence and goodness of heart; but the young women were objects of particular admiration; tall, robust, and well formed, their faces beaming with smiles, and unruffled good humour, but wearing a degree of modesty and bashfulness that would do honour to the most virtuous nation on earth. Their teeth, like ivory, were regular and beautiful, without a single exception; and all of them, both male and female, had the most marked English features.

We are told, moreover, in the pleasing account given in the Quarterly Review of that date:—

"They sometimes wreathe caps or bonnets for the head, in the most tasty manner, to protect the face from the rays of the sun; and though, as Captain Pipon observes, they have only had the instruction of their Otaheitan mothers, 'our dressmakers in London would be delighted with the simplicity, and yet elegant taste, of these untaught females.'

"Their native modesty, assisted by a proper sense of religion and morality, instilled into their youthful minds by John Adams, had hitherto preserved these interesting people pure and uncorrupted.

"They all labour, while young, in the cultivation of the ground; and when possessed of a sufficient quantity of cleared land,

and of stock to maintain a family, they are allowed to marry, but always with the consent of Adams.

"The greatest harmony prevailed in this little society; their only quarrels, and these rarely happened, being, according to their own expression, *quarrels of the mouth;* they are honest in their dealings, which consist of bartering different articles for mutual accommodation.

"Their habitations are extremely neat. The little village of Pitcairn forms a pretty square, the houses at the upper end of which are occupied by the patriarch John Adams and his family, consisting of his old blind wife and three daughters, from fifteen to eighteen years of age, and a boy of eleven; a daughter of his wife by a former husband, and a son-in-law. On the opposite side is the dwelling of Thursday October Christian, and in the centre is a smooth verdant lawn, on which the poultry are let loose, fenced in so as to prevent the intrusion of the domestic quadrupeds. All that was done was obviously undertaken on a settled plan, unlike to anything to be met with on the other islands.

JOHN ADAMS'S HOUSE, BUILT BY HIMSELF.

In their houses they had a good deal of decent furniture, consisting of beds laid upon bedsteads, with neat covering; they had also tables, and large chests to contain their valuables and clothing, which is made from the bark of a certain tree, prepared chiefly by the elder Otaheitan females. Adams's house consisted of two rooms, and the windows had shutters to pull to at night. The younger part of the sex are, as before stated, employed with their brothers, under the direction of Adams, in the culture of the ground, which produced cocoa-nuts, bananas, the bread-fruit-tree, yams, sweet potatoes, and turnips. They have also plenty of hogs and goats; the woods abound with a species of wild hog, and the coasts of the island with several kinds of good fish.

"Their agricultural implements are made by themselves, from the iron supplied by the *Bounty*, which, with great labour, they beat out into spades, hatchets, &c. This was not all. The old man kept a regular journal, in which was entered the nature and quantity of work performed by each family, what each had received, and what was due on account.

There was, it seemed, besides private property, a sort of general stock, out of which articles were issued on account to the several members of the community; and for mutual accommodation, exchanges of one kind of provision for another were very frequent, as salt for fresh provisions, vegetables and fruit for poultry, fish, &c.; also, when the stores of one family were low, or wholly expended, a fresh supply was raised from another, or out of the general stock, to be repaid when circumstances were more favourable." *

The name of John Adams is so closely identified with Pitcairn's Island, and so much of the present happy state of the people is owing, under the Divine blessing, to him, that it is difficult to say too much on this part of the subject. The description given by Captain Beechey of Adams, as well as of the young islanders, who came out in a boat to the *Blossom*, when off the island in December 1825, is so graphic, that it must be quoted in his own words:—

"They sprang up the side, and shook every

* See Quarterly Review, vol. iii. p. 378, &c.

officer by the hand, with undisguised feelings of gratification. The activity of the young men outstripped that of old Adams, who was, consequently, almost the last to greet us. He was unusually strong and active for his age, notwithstanding the inconvenience of considerable corpulency. He was dressed in a sailor's shirt and trowsers, and a low-crowned hat, which he instinctively held in his hand until desired to put it on. He still retained his sailor's gait, doffing his hat, and smoothing down his bald forehead whenever he was addressed by the officers. It was the first time he had been on board a ship of war since the mutiny, and his mind naturally reverted to scenes which could not fail to produce a temporary embarrassment, heightened, perhaps, by the familiarity with which he found himself addressed by persons of a class with those whom he had been accustomed to obey. Apprehension for his safety formed no part of his thoughts: he had received too many demonstrations of the good feeling that existed towards him, both on the part of the British Government and of individuals, to entertain any alarm on that head; and as every person endeavoured to set his mind at rest, he very soon made himself at home.

"The young men, ten in number, were tall, robust, and healthy, with good-natured countenances which would anywhere have procured them a friendly reception; and with a simplicity of manner and a fear of doing wrong, which at once prevented the possibility of giving offence. Unacquainted with the world, they asked a number of questions, which would have applied better to persons with whom they had been intimate, and who had left them but a short time before, than to perfect strangers; and inquired after ships and people we had never heard of. Their dress, made up of the presents which had been given them by the masters and seamen of merchant ships, was a perfect caricature. Some had on long black coats, without any other article of dress, except trowsers; some, shirts without coats; and others, waistcoats without either; none had shoes or stockings, and only two possessed hats, neither of which seemed likely to hang long together."

The following picture of filial affection, drawn by a careful and intelligent observer, is well worthy of insertion. Captain Beechey, anxious to visit the houses at Pitcairn, rather than pass another night at sea, determined to put off with some of his men in boats, and to accompany Adams and the islanders on shore. He says:—"The difficulty of landing was more than repaid by the friendly reception we met with on the beach from Hannah Young, a very interesting young woman, the daughter of Adams. It appeared that John Buffett, who was a seafaring man, ascertained the ship was a man-of-war, and, not knowing exactly why, became so alarmed for the safety of Adams, that he either could not, or would not, answer any of the interrogations which were put to him. This mysterious silence set all the party in tears, as they feared he had discovered something adverse to their patriarch. At length his obduracy yielded to their entreaties; but before he explained the cause of his conduct, the boats were seen to put off from the ship, and Hannah immediately hurried to the beach to kiss the old man's cheek, which she did with a fervency demonstrative of the warmest affection."

Captain Beechey observes, that Adams on no occasion neglected his usual devotions. The old man, while on board the *Blossom*, slept in that officer's cabin, in a retired corner of which he fell on his knees each night, to say his prayers, and was always up first in the morning for the same purpose. Captain Beechey, who made many highly valuable notes respecting the character and customs of the people twenty-seven years since, gives the following remarkable account of them:—

"During the whole time I was with them I never heard them indulge in a joke, or other levity; and the practice of it is apt to give offence. They are so accustomed to take what is said in its literal meaning, that irony was always considered a falsehood in spite of explanation. They could not see the propriety of uttering what was not strictly true for any purpose whatever. The sabbath-day is devoted entirely to prayer, reading, and serious meditation. No boat is allowed to quit the shore, nor any work whatever to be done, cooking excepted, for which preparation is made the preceding evening. I attended their church on this day, and found the service well conducted. The prayers were read by Adams, and the lessons by Buffett; the service being preceded by hymns. The greatest devotion was apparent in every individual, and in the children there was a seriousness unknown in the younger part of our communities at home. In the course of the Litany they prayed for their sovereign and all the royal family with much apparent loyalty and sincerity. Some family prayers, which were thought appropriate to their particular case, were added to the usual service, and Adams, fearful of leaving out any essential part, read in addition those prayers which are intended only as substitutes for others. A sermon followed, which was very well delivered by Buffett; and lest any part of it should be forgotten, or escape attention, it was read three times. The whole concluded with hymns, which were first sung by the grown people, and afterwards by the children. The service thus performed was very long; but the neat and cleanly appearance of the congregation, the devotion that animated every countenance, and the innocence and simplicity of the little children, prevented the attendance from becoming wearisome. In about half an hour afterwards we again assembled to prayers. They may be said to have church five times on a Sunday.

"All that remains to be said of these excellent people is, that they appear to live together in perfect harmony and contentment; to be virtuous, religious, cheerful and hospitable beyond the limits of prudence; to be patterns of conjugal and parental affection, and to have very few vices. We remained with them many days, and their unreserved manners gave us the fullest opportunity of becoming acquainted with any faults they might have possessed." *

In the year 1830, the Hon. W. Waldegrave, Captain of H. M. S. *Seringapatam*, touched at Pitcairn's Island. The following extracts from a letter of this officer, now Earl Waldegrave, will show that the moral and

* Captain F. W. Beechey's "Narrative of a Voyage to the Pacific and Behring's Straits;" a work of much interest.

religious training of the rising generation had been well attended to subsequently to John Adams's death :—

"Pitcairn's Island, March 17, 1830.

"On the 15th of March I landed at this island, and was friendly and hospitably received by George Nobbs, and all the inhabitants. My officers and men were most kindly treated at breakfast and dinner, and slept in their houses. My crew received a supply of cocoa-nuts and fruits. I had the gratification to hear William Quintal say part of the Catechism, and answer several questions as to his knowledge of the redemption in Christ, and of the different habits of the Jews, their sects and diseases, perfectly, clearly, and distinctly; showing that he understood their meaning. I also heard two little girls repeat part of a hymn, which showed to me how well they had been instructed; and lastly, I attended at their evening prayers. I can only trust that the God who preserves this island and its inhabitants from foreign injury, may keep them alive in the true faith of Jesus Christ, in purity and peace, so that each person, at his death, may quit this world in the expectation of being for ever in heaven, through the merits of Jesus Christ. It was with very great satisfaction that I observed the Christian simplicity of these natives. They appeared to have no guile. Their cottages were open to all, and all were welcome to their food; the pig, the fowl, was killed and dressed instantly; the beds were ready; each was willing to show any and every part of the island. Before they began a meal, all joined hands in the attitude of prayer, with eyes raised to heaven, and one recited a simple grace, grateful for the present food, but beseeching spiritual nourishment. Each answered, Amen, and after a pause the meal began. At the conclusion, another grace was offered up. Should any one arrive during the repast, all ceased to eat. The new guest said grace, to which each repeated, Amen, and then the meal continued."

There having been the fear of a dearth of water at Pitcairn in 1831, the people, eighty-seven in number, were removed from the island, by order of the British Government, in the barque *Lucy Anne*, sent from Sydney, New South Wales. On being landed at Otaheite on March 23d, they were well received by Queen Pomaré.

Captain Sandilands, of H.M.'s ship *Comet*, in his despatch to Rear-Admiral Sir E. W. Owen, K.C.B. gave an interesting report of this case of emigration, and of the manner in which the voyagers were welcomed by Queen Pomaré, who was then, and is still, the ruling sovereign of Otaheite. At her Majesty's desire, Captain Sandilands landed the people of Pitcairn at her residence, about three miles from the anchorage, where houses were provided for them, until she gave up for their temporary use a large dwelling belonging to herself in the town of Papiété. A tract of rich land was also marked out, as a desirable territory for their future residence. Having assembled the chiefs of the district, the Queen, in a speech, formally announced that she had assigned this land to her guests from Pitcairn, giving directions at the same time that her people should immediately commence the construction of houses for the new-comers. In showing this hospitality, she appears to have consulted her own kind disposition, and also to have endeavoured to fulfil the promises given by her father, the late King Pomaré who had promised them welcome and protection in case of need. Nor was this good feeling confined to the Queen. Much regard was generally shown by the Otaheitans, who sought out with diligence, whether there might not be relations among their guests. In one instance a woman came a considerable distance, and discovered in one of the four remaining women a long-absent sister.

The fact of Queen Pomaré having been engaged in a troublesome civil war at the time of the visit of the Islanders, places her kindness and attention to them in a still more pleasing light.

This is the Queen Pomaré, who, early in 1843, complained to her Majesty, Queen Victoria, of the proceedings of the French, in threatening her peace and government. There is much pathos and simplicity in the Otaheitan Queen's mode of address to her "Sister and Friend." The following are extracts from her letter literally translated :—

"Tahiti, January 23, 1843.

"My dear Friend and Sister, Queen Victoria, Queen of Great Britain,—Health and peace to you! And saved made you be by Jehovah, the Foundation of our power as Queens of our respective countries. We dwell in peace by the arrangements made by our predecessors.

"This is my speech to you, my sister friend. Commiserate me in my affliction, in my helplessness, in which my nation is involved with France.

"The existing protectorate government of France in my dominions I do not acknowledge. I knew nothing of what my chiefs and the French Consul had done before I wrote to you by Captain Jones, I being absent at Raiaté."

After bemoaning the dependent state into which she had been thrown by French intervention, and the political movements of her chiefs, she proceeds:—

"And now, my friend, think of me, have compassion on me, and assist me; let it be powerful, let it be timely, and saving, that I may be reinstated in my government.

"Have compassion on me in my present trouble, in my affliction, and great helplessness. Do not cast me away, assist me quickly, my friend. I run to you for refuge, to be covered under your great shadow, the same as afforded to my fathers by your fathers, who are now dead, and whose kingdoms have descended to us the weaker vessels.

"I renew that agreement. Let it be lasting and for ever. Let its continuance extend not only to ourselves and children, but to our children's children. My friend, do not by any means separate our friendship. This is my true wish.

"I now deliver up to you, my friend, my last effort. My only hope of being restored is in you. Be quick to help me, for I am nearly dead. I am like a captive pursued by a warrior and nearly taken, whose spear is close to me. The time is very nigh, when I fear I shall lose my government and my land.

"My friend, send quickly a large ship of war to assist me. A French ship of war is daily expected here. Speedily send a ship of war to protect me, and I shall be saved. It is my wish that the Admiral may speedily come to Tahiti. If he cannot speedily come, I wish a large ship of war may come just at this present time.

"Continually send here your ships of war. Let not one month pass away without one, until all my present difficulties are over.

"I have also at this time written a letter to your Admiral in the Spanish coast, to come to Tahiti and assist me. Health and peace to you! may you be blessed, my sister friend, Queen of Great Britain, &c.

"POMARÉ,
"*Queen of Tahiti.*"

Queen Pomaré, however, and her people were doomed to feel the power of the French, who have erected a fort, commanding the entrance to the harbour of Otaheite. They have a frigate and a war steamer anchored there, and a military force on the island. The queen, who is now upwards of fifty years of age, is married; and although she has children of her own, she adopted Reuben Nobbs, the Pastor's eldest son; but she did not remove him from the care of his parents.

CHAPTER V.

RETURN OF THE PITCAIRN EMIGRANTS TO THEIR ISLAND IN 1833—PRESENT POPULATION OF PITCAIRN—LOYALTY OF THE ISLANDERS—THEIR RULES AND CUSTOMS—THE ISLANDERS' DAY AT PITCAIRN—RECEPTION OF VESSELS TOUCHING AT THE ISLAND—HOSPITALITY TO STRANGERS.

To return to the Pitcairn emigrants at Otaheite. Their health suffered in the new climate, and the dissipation of the place proved distasteful to a well-ordered Christian community. It was owing, partly to this, and partly to the love of country, which is a powerful principle at Pitcairn, that the people soon found their way back to their own home. When the British ship, *Challenger*, touched at Otaheite in 1833, it was found, that all whom death had spared had returned to the island of Pitcairn. Some had yielded to the temptations to intemperance. Sickness also had become prevalent among them, and had carried off twelve; and five died almost immediately after their return.

No real grounds having existed for the clearance of Pitcairn in 1831, very serious consideration will doubtless be given to the subject, before any plans are projected for the removal of the inhabitants from this island to another, on the presumed score of necessity. Should there be scarcity, and want of room, in consequence of the increase of population, it would surely not be necessary to remove all the islanders. Mr. Nobbs has said, in the hearing of the author, that as long as two families should remain at Pitcairn, he would remain also. Captain Fanshawe, of the *Daphne*, who visited the islanders in 1849, observed, "I could not trace in any of them the slightest desire to remove elsewhere. On the contrary, they expressed the greatest repugnance to do so, whilst a sweet potato remained to them; a repugnance much enhanced by their emigration to Otaheite about eighteen years ago."

If found needful, a certain amount of emigration might surely take place, formed on the principle of serving the interests of others, as well as their own, by means of Christian instruction and example: and the good leaven, thus infused into other communities, would produce the happiest effects upon them.

In the little work, entitled, "The Mutiny of the Bounty," it is remarked, that the Pitcairners have already proceeded from the simple canoe to row-boats; and that the progress from this to small-decked vessels is simple and natural. They may thus, at some future period, be the means of spreading Christianity, and, consequently, civilization, throughout the numerous groups of islands in the Southern Pacific.

By the last account in the autumn of 1852, the number of persons inhabiting the island was 170; namely, 88 males, and 82 females. All are natives of the plaçe except three, the Rev. Geo. H. Nobbs, John Buffett, and John Evans. The only surnames on the island are eight; namely, Adams, Christian, M'Coy, Quintal, Young, Buffett, Evans, and Nobbs. Brown, Martin, and Williams, had no children; nor had any of the Otaheitan men. John Mills left no son.

The original division of the island was into nine parts, between the nine mutineers; it is now subdivided into twenty-one, the present number of families. Some little misunderstandings occasionally arise as to boundaries; but these, as well as such other matters of dispute as now and then occur, are generally soon settled by the chief magistrate, and the two councillors.

The owners of "this sceptred isle,"

"This precious stone set in the silver sea,"

avow a hearty allegiance to the Queen of England. Her Majesty's birth-day is observed as an occasion of much joy. All the people assemble near the church in holiday apparel; the bell is set ringing, and old and young unite in singing loyal songs in honour of the day. Not only the cheerful bell is heard, but it has been usual to introduce the deep-mouthed gun to assist at the solemnity. The history of this gun is curious. It once belonged to the *Bounty*, and was fished up from the bottom of the sea in 1845, with one of its companions which had been spiked, and which was therefore useless. The better of the two, after remaining many fathom deep for five-and-fifty years, is somewhat honey-combed, and, when brought into play, is used with requisite caution.* The scene presented by the assemblage of the people on the Queen's birthday has been depicted by a poet of their own. The following stanzas by Mr. Nobbs, in one of his national songs, produce a pleasing sketch:—

Ha! that flash yon grove illuming,
  Long impervious to the sun;
Now the quick report comes booming
  From the ocean-rescued gun.

Now the bell is gaily ringing,
  Where yon white-robed train is seen;
Now they all unite in singing
  GOD PRESERVE OUR GRACIOUS QUEEN.

In the year 1849, a Frenchman, of a military air, and partly military costume, arriving, with some other travellers, from the brig *Fanny*, was courteously received by the islanders. With the politeness characteristic of his countrymen, he soon engaged in conversation with Mr. Nobbs, and, in imperfect English, inquired, Whether the people of Pitcairn had heard of Prince Louis Napoleon, and the French Republic? and, as the next

* Since these words appeared in the first edition, intelligence has been received of a melancholy accident, occasioned by the incautious use of this gun, (page 273.)

CHURCH AND SCHOOL-HOUSE, PITCAIRN.

question, Would they enlist themselves under it? Suiting the action to the word, he took a paper for signatures from his pocket.

He was briefly answered by Mr. Nobbs's quietly pointing to the English flag, which waved in the wind over their heads;

> "The flag that braved a thousand years,
> The battle and the breeze!"

The Pastor then assured him, that they knew all about Louis Napoleon, and the French Republic; but that all the people on the island were faithful subjects of Victoria, Queen of England. The Frenchman again bowed, begged pardon, returned the paper to his pocket, and explained, that "he did not know Pitcairn was a colony."

Though it is not a colony, it is entirely English; and such a loyal and united community, as a whole, cannot be found in any of the colonies or dependencies of the British empire. The English union-jack is hoisted on all grand occasions; and to England the people would look for protection, should any attempt be made to disturb their position. But who would think of disturbing so inoffensive and so poor a settlement?

Their leading man is a magistrate, who is elected on the first of January every year, by a general vote of males and females who have attained the age of eighteen years. Married persons, both males and females, though they may be under that age, are entitled to vote. Two councillors are chosen at the same time, one elected by the magistrate, the other by the people. When there is any dispute to be settled, which cannot well be decided by the magistrate, or by the magistrate and councillors combined, a jury of seven is called, to whom the matter is referred. Then should the matter not be satisfactorily arranged, it stands over until the arrival of a British man-of-war; and there is no appeal against the Captain's decision. During the interval the matter drops, and no ill-feeling remains.

It is a principle with them, never to let the sun go down upon their wrath.

What an example is conveyed in the practical adherence to this scriptural rule! How simple and effectual a mode of adjusting differences, and preventing the growth of all uncharitableness!

"The wise will let their anger cool,
At least before 'tis night;
But in the bosom of a fool
It burns till morning-light."

The office of magistrate is not coveted: it being in some respects an invidious one. It sometimes happens, that the respected individual for whom this honour is designed would, rather than accept it, kill a hog for the public good. The duties of the magistracy are always fulfilled without fear, favour, or affection.

With respect to the general appearance of the islanders, in their features and complexion, as well as their dress and manners, they are said to resemble the people of one of our English villages of the better order. A few of them are, however, rather darker than the generality of Europcans, partaking more of their half-Otaheitan descent.

A few words about dress. The women generally wear a full petticoat, and over that a loose gown, with a handkerchief thrown over the shoulders. A wreath of flowers is often worn round the head. There are many large trees on the island, which produce small white flowers, much esteemed for their fragrance; and of the flowers of this tree (*Morinda citrifolia*), or a mixture of them with bright red flowers, the females make their wreaths. Their hair is worn in bands, and is brought up in a very becoming manner into a knot cleverly twisted behind.

The men wear short trowsers, the legs of which are cut off two or three inches above the knee. A shirt, and a cap or hat, complete their costume. They seldom wear shoes or stockings, except on Sundays.

The people live principally on vegetables, having meat about once a-week; and each family gets fish once, and, occasionally, twice a-week. The fishing is difficult and precarious, as they have to seek the fish in very deep water, often at the depth of 150 or 200 fathoms.

At the commencement of the yam-digging season, in April, when there is much hard work in prospect, and they require better food, and more of it, each family, having a hog, kills it. This is the period for the people to indulge, beyond their usual custom, in animal food.

There are three burial-places on the island. The funerals are always attended by every member of the community, even if the deceased should be but an infant.

The children are early instructed in swimming; and many of their sports are in the water. They also learn to thread the difficult passes of the rocks like so many young goats. The personal strength and activity of the men, as described by Captain Beechey, as he observed them in 1825, do not seem to be diminished at the present day. Lieutenant Belcher, mentioned in the subjoined extract, is now Captain Sir Edward Belcher, C.B., who has gone out in H.M.S. *Assistance*, to the North Seas, in search of the missing crews of Sir John Franklin.

"Two of the strongest on the island, George Young, and Edward Quintal, have each carried at one time, without inconvenience, a kedge anchor, two sledge hammers, and an armourer's anvil, amounting to upwards of six hundredweight. Quintal, at another time, carried a boat twenty-eight feet in length. Their activity on land has been already mentioned. I shall merely give another instance, which was supplied by Lieut. Belcher, who was admitted to be the most active among the officers on board, and who did not consider himself behindhand in such exploits. He offered to accompany one of the natives down a difficult descent, in spite of the warning given by his friend, that he was unequal to the task. They, however, commenced the perilous descent; but Mr. Belcher was obliged to confess his inability to proceed, while his companion, perfectly assured of his own footing, offered him his hand, and said he would conduct him to the bottom, if he would depend on him for safety. In the water they are almost as much at home as on land, and can remain nearly a whole day in the sea. They frequently swam round their little island. When the sea beat heavily on the island, they have plunged into the breakers and swum to sea beyond them. This they sometimes did, pushing a barrel of water before them when it could be got off in no other way; and in this manner we procured several tons of water without a single cask being stove."

The Rev. Wm. Armstrong, late Chaplain

at Valparaiso, in a letter to the author, from that place, dated October 1849, stated that an English man-of-war, the *Pandora*, had lately arrived direct from Pitcairn's, and that the commander, Lieut. Wood, and the officers, had given the most pleasing account of the happy state in which their little community were living. They were described as a remarkably strong and healthy people. For instance, a young woman, eighteen years of age, had been accustomed to carry on her shoulders a hundred pounds weight of yams over hills and precipitous places, and for a considerable distance, where one unaccustomed to such exercise would scarcely be able to scramble. A man, sixty years old, with ease carried the surgeon of the *Pandora* up a steep ascent from the landing-place, which he had himself in vain attempted to mount, the ground being very slippery from recent rains; and the officer being a large man, six feet high, rendered it the more surprising. Indeed, Lieut. Wood said he was himself borne aloft in the arms of a damsel, and carried up the hill with the utmost facility.

From the date of the first intelligence respecting the inhabitants of Pitcairn, there has been no variation in the character given of them. As they were, in purity and peace, those two great essentials of human happiness, when Sir Thomas Staines visited the island, in 1814, so they are now, in 1853,—the same contented, kind, and God-fearing race. Nor need we feel surprise at this, however delighted we may be with the picture. They are sensible of the treasure which they possess in the Bible, and take it for their guide in the performance of their duty towards God, and their neighbour. And they have learned to estimate the value and excellency of the Book of Common Prayer, which, as a faithful exponent of the revealed word of God, has tended to keep them "in the unity of faith, in the bond of peace, and in righteousness of life."

The difficulty of landing on the island, and the want of harbour and anchorage, though at first sight a disadvantage, may have proved a blessing, in preserving these simple-minded people from the baneful effects too likely to arise from crews remaining, as a matter of course, among them. As it is, the behaviour both of officers and men who visit the place, is stated to be most exemplary. No encouragement is given to evil; and no instance can be quoted of the transgression, on the part of visiters, of the sacred law of hospitality. On the contrary, the good habits, and moral and religious conduct of the islanders, do not fail to produce, by the power of example, a wholesome influence on strangers.

If it be asked, how the people pass their time, and what they can have to do in a spot, whose utmost limit is barely four miles and a half in circumference, comprising less of extent than Hyde Park and Kensington Gardens, put together, the question may be answered by a description of the Pitcairn Islanders' ordinary day.

They rise early, generally as soon as it is light. As the difference of longitude between England and Pitcairn is about 130 degrees, or nearly nine hours in time, at seven in the morning with them, it is about four in the afternoon with us. Each house has early family prayer, preceded by Scripture reading; two chapters of the Bible being generally selected for the morning, and one for the evening. After some slight refreshment, for they have only two regular meals a day, the business of the Pitcairners' day begins.

The young people are sent to school, in pursuance of a law of the island; and after the "graver hours, that bring constraint, and sweeten liberty," they have their needful food, and their childish amusements. They are fond of flying kites, and of games at ball; though the want of room on the island imposes a limit on the nature and number of the out-of-door diversions both of young and old.

The occupation of the men consists in cultivating their land; looking after their gardens; building and improving their houses, which are neat, clean, and commodious; rearing stock; fencing in their plantations; manufacturing hats from the leaf of the palm; making fancy boxes, &c., which they keep in store for barter with whalers, or other vessels which may call at Pitcairn for refreshment.

At about twelve o'clock they have a plain and substantial breakfast, or dinner, consisting of yams and potatoes, made into a kind of bread, for which they do not fail to ask God's blessing, and to render Him thanks.

> "O Hand of bounty, largely spread,
> By whom our every want is fed;
> Whate'er we touch, or taste, or see,
> We owe them all, O Lord, to Thee."
>
> HEBER.

So strict is their observance of the duty of saying grace before and after meals, that "we do not know," says Captain Beechey, "of any instance in which it has been forgotten. On one occasion I had engage Adams in conversation, and he incautiously took the first mouthful without having said his grace; but, before he had swallowed it, he recollected himself, and, feeling as if he had committed a crime, immediately put away what he had in his mouth, and commenced his prayer."

Fishing for a kind of cod, grey mullet, and red snapper, though no very hopeful pursuit in the deep water round the island, occasionally forms part of the day's employment; nor of the day only; for sometimes they go forth at night among the rocks close to the sea, or row out in a canoe, and, taking a light, attract the fish, which they strike with a pole, armed with five barbed prongs, and so take.

Suppose, however, the islander returned from his day's labour to his supper, at about seven o'clock in the evening. Except once or twice a-week, no fish, meat, or poultry will be found to grace the board, but yams, and sweet potatoes, and such humble fare as has been prepared by the females of the family. For the women have their daily tasks to perform; some preparing the ground, taking up yams, and doing other work requiring diligence and strength. There being no servants, the wives or daughters make and mend the clothes, and attend to all the requisite household affairs. They also manufacture *tappa*, or native cloth, from the bark of the "anti," or paper-mulberry, which is rolled up, and soaked in water, and then beaten out with wooden mallets, and spread forth to dry. The author has in his possession a piece of beautifully wrought white tappa, given him by Mrs. Heywood, and bearing a label, which states that it was made by the wife of Fletcher Christian, from the bark of the paper-mulberry-tree. The piece from which this portion was taken, was given by her, when at a very advanced age, *for Peter's wife*, to Captain Jenkin Jones, when he visited the island, in Her Majesty's ship *Curaçoa*, in 1841.

The cooking is performed by the females. Their cooking-places are apart from their dwellings; and there are no fireplaces in any of the houses. Baked, not roasted, meats are the substantial luxuries of the table at Pitcairn. Their ovens, like those at Otaheite, described by Captain Cook, are formed with stones in the ground. Captain Beechey says, that an oven is made in the ground, sufficiently large to contain a good-sized pig, and is lined throughout with stones nearly equal in size. These, having been made as hot as possible, are covered with some broad leaves, generally of the ti-plant, and on them is placed the meat. If it be a pig, its inside is lined with heated stones, as well as the oven. Such vegetables as are to accompany the meal are then placed round the meat that is to be dressed. The whole is covered with leaves of the ti-plant, and buried beneath a heap of earth, straw, or rushes and boughs, which by a little use become matted into one mass. In about an hour and a quarter, the meat is sufficiently cooked.

There is much wisdom in the arrangement, regarding the absence of fireplaces from their wooden cottages. They are also sparing in their use of lights in general. They have no candles, but use oil, and torches made with nuts of the Doodoe-tree (*aleurites triloba*). They have no glass for the windows. The shutters, which serve the purpose of admitting light and air, are closed in bad weather. For the most part pure water, but, now and then, tea, constitutes their drink. Cocoa-nut milk, and water sweetened with syrup, extracted from the bruised sugar-cane, vary the drinks of these temperate people. No wines or spirits are admitted in the island, except in small quantities for medicinal purposes. The water which they use does not come from springs, (there are none in the island,) but from reservoirs, or tanks, neatly excavated, which collect the rain. Of these there are five or six, holding from three to four thousand gallons of water each, sufficient not only for the consumption of the inhabitants, but for supplies to whalers, and other vessels.

With respect to literary occupation, "You will be glad to hear," wrote Mr. Armstrong to the author, "that they are all well educated. The young men are instructed in navigation, and some of the lower branches of mathematics. They all live together in the greatest harmony, and in the strictest observance of religious duties—public, family, and private—with every appearance of perfect freedom from all crime, and bearing the stamp of extreme innocence and simplicity.

"A new regulation has been recently made for the distribution of all their books among the families,—they having been before kept as public property,—as it was believed they would be more read and valued in that way; and for which purpose shelves have been put up in all their houses, which are very neat and comfortable, though more like ship-cabins than dwelling-houses. The reason they give for this arrangement is, that they are in the habit of walking into each other's houses with the same freedom as into their own, and, taking up a book, will sit down and read it aloud, or not, as they feel disposed. The books of the *Society for Promoting Christian Knowledge* reached them in good time, some of which were particularly suitable; there being several copies of the same work, such as the Homilies, and others."

With the employment found by the inhabitants, in the ways of industry above described, and the advantage and amusement derived from reading—for they have many books of general literature, as well as publications of a directly religious character—the day cannot be said to hang heavy on hand in Pitcairn's Island.

> "How various his employment whom the world
> Calls idle, and who justly in return
> Esteems that busy world an idler too!
> Friends, books, a garden, and perhaps his pen,
> Delightful industry enjoy'd at home,
> And nature in her cultivated trim
> Dress'd to his taste, inviting him abroad—
> Can he want occupation who has these?
> Will he be idle who has much t' enjoy?
> A life all turbulence and noise may seem.
> To him that leads it, wise, and to be praised;
> But wisdom is a pearl, with most success
> Sought in still water, and beneath clear skies."
>
> COWPER.

When the shades of evening draw on, the islanders, one and all, again remember Him, who is about their path and about their bed, and spieth out all their ways. Nor are they slow to acknowledge His claims, who expects the grateful homage of His intelligent creatures, and whose protection and blessing they beg in family worship, before they lie down to sleep. And then, without any thought of locks, bolts, or bars,—for they have no such defences, nor any need of them,—each may feel at night a happy confidence in the protection and blessing of that gracious Lord, who has guided and preserved them through the day.

"Guarded by Thee, I lay me down,
My sweet repose to take;
For I through Thee securely sleep,
Through Thee in safety wake."

But if they are active and cheerful on common days, how great is their pleasure on descrying from the "Look-out Ridge" of their sea-girt rock, a sail on the edge of the horizon. How different are the feelings of the present islanders from those which possessed the inhabitants fifty or sixty years since! Then they sought a place of concealment, when they perceived a vessel heave in sight; now they rejoice at her approach.

A short account of the reception of a ship on their shores will interest the reader.

It is customary for each family, in turn, to have the privilege of receiving as their guest the captain of any vessel, whether a man-of-war or a whaler, which may happen to arrive. On her appearance sufficiently near, the master of the house, whose turn it is to be the host, goes off in a canoe, and, after satisfactory answers to questions as to the health of those on board, he ascends the ship's side; the canoe, which is but a light affair, being quickly hauled up after him. Most important are these inquiries; for if the small-pox, or any other infectious disorder, should find its way into the island, dreadful, indeed, would be the result. But when it is "all right," the ship's boat being lowered, the captain, and five or six men, conducted by the islander, who steers in the difficult parts, proceed to Bounty Bay. Some persons are always ready on the rocks to give a signal for the safe entrance of the boat, without which precaution serious accidents would frequently occur.

The captain and his company, attended by a number of the natives, who have descended from the village to the little beach, now ascend the hill, and generally walk first to the school-house, where they obtain a sight of the island-register, and examine the shipping-list, in which they enter the name of their own vessel; whence she has come, and whither she is bound. After some preliminary conversation, the representatives of the several families, one at least from each house, assemble; and after a hearty welcome, and the interchange of friendly expressions, inquire what is wanted for the vessel, as to vegetables, refreshments, &c. A list is handed in of the articles in demand, such as yams, sweet potatoes, &c., the price of these goods being always the same in time of scarcity as of plenty. The inhabitants then, in their turn, inquire of the captain, what he has to dispose of. This is generally found to be coarse cotton cloths, soap, oil, &c. with perhaps some small quantities of lead, or iron. While the captain is engaged in conversation with the teacher, on matters of mutual and general interest, the health of the Queen being the first in the series of questions and answers, the inhabitants retire, and consult among themselves what each person's proportion of the captain's wants amounts to. This being settled, each repairs to his own plantation to procure his part, which, in every instance, is, as far as possible, an equal share from each family.

Such is the reliance placed by visiters on the honesty and integrity of the islanders, that in no case does the captain think it necessary, either himself, or by proxy, to be present at the measurement of the articles required. One of the islanders is appointed to remain at the market-place, to take an account of the things sent on board; and the mode of dealing is always cheerfully acceded to by the authorities of the vessel. The articles are removed from the market-place to Bounty Bay, where they are deposited, at the captain's risk, and from whence they are conveyed in boats; or, if the surf is heavy, the goods are packed in casks, which are conducted by the natives swimming with them through the heavy surf to the boats lying outside the broken water.

It is the custom on festive occasions, when the captain and his friends from the ship are entertained at dinner, for the women to attend upon the party at table. This is the exception to the general rule; as, usually, when there are no visiters, the men and women in a family sit down together. But the attendance of the females on strangers, and on their own relatives, has been misapprehended by some travellers as a mark of barbarism. Now, there must be some to wait; strangers must be hospitably served; and the younger women do these honours of their island in the most attentive and good-humoured manner. Here, again, the delicacy and good sense of the islanders are to be admired. It will be allowed that for husbands and brothers to be attending upon their female relatives and newly-landed guests, would be a less desirable and becoming mode than that at present adopted.

In March, 1850, five passengers of the barque *Noble*, Captain H. Parker, bound from New Zealand for California, were left by a mischance on Pitcairn; the vessel from which they had landed having been blown off from the island during the night. During the three weeks of their detention, which turned out to be a very agreeable visit, the strangers, who had no property about them but the clothes which they had on, received every mark of sympathy and friendship. One of these gentlemen, Mr. Walter Brodie, whom Mr. Nobbs entertained as his guest, employed himself chiefly in gathering materials for an account of the island and its hospitable inhabitants, which was afterwards published, and to which allusion has already been made.

Two of the other guests, the Baron de Thierry, and Mr. Hugh Carleton, especially the latter, applied themselves to the task of teaching the whole of the adult population to sing. Fortunately, the Baron happened to have a tuning-fork in his pocket; and the people, whose efforts in psalmody in church had been noticed as somewhat imperfect, caught with delight at the idea of a little musical instruction. "They proved," says Mr. Brodie, "remarkably intelligent, not one among the number being deficient in ear, while many had exceedingly fine voices. The progress surpassed the most sanguine expectations of the teacher. On the fourth day they sang through a catch in four parts with great steadiness. For people who had hitherto been unaware even of the existence in nature of *harmony*, the performance was very remarkable." Mr. Brodie has given the names of 57 pupils—being 30 males, and 27 females—as the "list of Carleton's musical class."

Hitherto their chief musical instrument in the church has been an accordion. But among the presents now designed for them is a capital small barrel and key organ, by Davison. This instrument has one row of keys, with a barrel to play ten of the best psalm and hymn tunes, and an octave and a half of pedals.

With regard to Mr. Brodie, it is worthy of remark, that though he had been thus detained at Pitcairn, he arrived in the barque *Colonist* at San Francisco, in California, twenty-eight days before the *Noble*, which had been ninety-three days from Pitcairn, the crew having suffered great privations from want of provision and water. His disappointment, which appeared so grievous, in missing his ship at Pitcairn, ended in his escaping the miseries to which the people in the *Noble* had been exposed, and in reckoning those few weeks in the island as among the happiest of his life.

J. A. Vinter, lith, from a daguerreotype Portrait by Mr. Kilburn. Day & Son, Lithrs

CHAPTER VI.

MR. NOBBS—SOME ACCOUNT OF HIS LIFE—TESTIMONIES TO HIS CHARACTER AND SERVICES—PROGRESS OF RELIGION IN THE ISLAND—SERVICES OF MR. NOBBS—REUBEN NOBBS—TESTIMONIES FROM THE REV. WM. ARMSTRONG AND CAPTAIN WORTH—LETTERS FROM THE ISLANDERS—STATE OF THE SCHOOL.

THE arrival of Mr. George Hunn Nobbs at Pitcairn's Island, in the year 1828, may be considered a providential occurrence for the well-being of the inhabitants. Admiral Moresby has remarked, that the success of twenty-four years' labour is an abundant proof, that, under the blessing of God, this faithful teacher has educated in the principles of our Church, as one united family, a community, whose simple and virtuous lives are so preeminent. A brief notice of his career, and of the circumstances which led him to the spot, cannot fail to be interesting, especially as he has now received the proper

J. A. Vinter, lith, from a daguerreotype Portrait by Mr Kilburn — Day & Son, Lithrs to The Q

George H Nobbs

CHAPTER VI.

MR. NOBBS—SOME ACCOUNT OF HIS LIFE—TESTIMONIES TO HIS CHARACTER AND SERVICES—PROGRESS OF RELIGION IN THE ISLAND—SERVICES OF MR. NOBBS—REUBEN NOBBS—TESTIMONIES FROM THE REV. WM. ARMSTRONG AND CAPTAIN WORTH—LETTERS FROM THE ISLANDERS—STATE OF THE SCHOOL.

THE arrival of Mr. George Hunn Nobbs at Pitcairn's Island, in the year 1828, may be considered a providential occurrence for the well-being of the inhabitants. Admiral Moresby has remarked, that the success of twenty-four years' labour is an abundant proof, that, under the blessing of God, this faithful teacher has educated in the principles of our Church, as one united family, a community, whose simple and virtuous lives are so preeminent. A brief notice of his career, and of the circumstances which led him to the spot, cannot fail to be interesting, especially as he has now received the proper sanction and authority to minister as a Clergyman of the Church of England.

Mr. Nobbs, who was born in Ireland in 1799, was in his youth a midshipman in the British navy, having first gone to sea when not much more than eleven years of age. He afterwards held a commission in the Chilian service under Lord Cochrane, now Earl of Dundonald, and became lieutenant in consequence of his services.

Among other important occurrences which took place during this period, and in which Mr. Nobbs bore a part, was the courageous enterprise of cutting out the Spanish frigate *Esmeralda*, of forty guns, which was lying in the bay, under the batteries of Callao, in Peru. The capture was accomplished late at night on the 5th of November, 1820. An address from Lord Cochrane had been delivered to the marines and seamen, which concluded with an injunction, that the Chilenos should act with valour, 'and that the English should do as they had always done, both in their own country, and elsewhere.' An account of this remarkable transaction, the success of which surpassed all that could have been imagined, is met with in Mrs. Graham's (afterwards Lady Callcott's) "Journal of a Residence in Chili in 1822."

Lieutenant Nobbs was also engaged in a severe conflict with a Spanish gun-brig near Arauco, a fortress of Chili; when in command of a gun-boat, after sustaining the loss of forty-eight men killed and wounded, out of a party of sixty-four, he was taken prisoner by the troops of the piratical Spanish general, Benevideis.

The prisoners were all shot, with the exception of Lieutenant Nobbs, and three English seamen. These four, after remaining for three weeks under sentence of death, were, quite unexpectedly, exchanged for four officers attached to Benevideis's army. Mr. Nobbs had seen his fellow-prisoners, from time to time, led out to be shot, and had heard the reports of the muskets consigning them to a dreadful death.

Lady Callcott states that Benevideis was the son of the inspector of a prison, and had been a foot-soldier in the first army of the Chilenos in the cause of South American independence. From her description of his

M

character and actions, the reader will infer, that Mr. Nobbs's rescue from his hands was indeed a providential event.

Having been made prisoner by the royalists, Benevideis entered their army, and, being taken soon after, was sent to be tried as a deserter; but he escaped by setting fire to the hut in which he was confined, and soon distinguished himself among the royalists by his talents and bravery. Again he was taken prisoner, and sentenced to be shot in company with many others. He fell with the rest; but, though thought to have been executed, was not killed; and he afterwards joined the patriots. Being, however, suspected and accused by their general, San Martin, of treachery, he once more turned against them; and hence arose the atrocities with which Benevideis is charged. He murdered his prisoners in cold blood; and his great delight was to invite the captured officers to an elegant entertainment, and after they had eaten and drank, march them into his court-yard, while he stood at the window to see them shot. Some, to whom he had promised safety, he delivered over to the Indians, whose cruel customs with regard to prisoners of war he well knew; and they were cruelly murdered.

His cause having failed, he fitted out a privateer, to provide himself with food and ammunition; and at length, on the 1st of February, 1822, finding that he could hold out no longer, he attempted to escape to one of the Spanish ports in a small boat; but he was recognised, seized, and sent to Santiago, where, on the 21st, he was tried, and sentenced to death. On the 23d he was dragged from prison, tied to the tail of a mule, and then hanged in the palace square.

Mr. Nobbs, having quitted the Chilian service, after many hardships and dangers, took passage to England in 1822, in the ship *Elizabeth*, which had shortly before touched at Pitcairn's Island. The commander of that ship, in the course of conversation, expatiated so frequently on the happiness of the people at Pitcairn, that Mr. Nobbs seriously intended to go thither, if his life should be spared; and he set out, with this object in view, in the beginning of 1826. His wish was to lead a life of peace and usefulness to his fellow-creatures. He had at that period been four times round the world: and he left England with the full and avowed intention of going to Pitcairn's Island. He was detained for a long time in Calcutta; from whence, after a very narrow escape from shipwreck in the Straits of Sunda, he crossed the Pacific to Valparaiso. There, and afterwards at Callao, he suffered a further detention; but ultimately he succeeded in leaving Callao in a frail bark of eighteen tons burden, having expended one hundred and fifty pounds sterling on the vessel and her outfit. He was accompanied by only one other person, an American, named Noah Bunker, and arrived at Pitcairn in October 1828. His companion died soon afterwards; and the vessel afforded the materials for a house for Mr. Nobbs. John Adams received him with kindness; and after Adams's death in March 1829, Mr. Nobbs, who had been engaged in keeping school from the period of his arrival, was appointed the teacher.

When he first entered upon his charge, the number of inhabitants was only sixty-eight. From that time he has been with them, through evil report and good report, as their pastor, surgeon, and schoolmaster, with the exception of a few months, when he was removed from the island, in consequence of the intrusion of a Mr. Joshua Hill, who arrived from Otaheite in 1832. This person, who was then about sixty years of age, informed the inhabitants that he had been authorized by the British Government to reside at Pitcairn's Island; when in fact he had received no such authority. Mr. Nobbs appears to have been of too plain and straightforward a character to suit this new-comer, whose presence amongst the people caused much trouble; as he divided their little society into two factions; one siding with him, the other with the constitution as it was. At length, partly by splendid promises, and partly by instilling into the simple minds around him the fear of giving offence to the Government at home, whom he affected to represent, he enlisted some of the natives against the three Europeans, and succeeded in excluding them and their families, for a time, from the island.

Certain misrepresentations concerning Mr. Nobbs, which are alluded to by Admiral Moresby, in his letter contained in the Preface, took their rise at about this time.

It is fortunate for any one who may have been misrepresented by Mr. Hill, that he wrote in June 1834 a long letter, full of himself and his own praises, which has been published,* and which sufficiently shows into what sort of hands the islanders of Pitcairn had fallen during the time of Hill's influence. The author cannot refrain from quoting a passage, as a specimen of this epistle :—

"I have visited the Falls of Niagara and Montmorency, the natural bridge in Virginia, the great Reciprocating Fountain in East Tennessee, the great Temple of Elephanta at Bombay. I have dined with a prince, as well as with a princess; and with a count, a baron, an ambassador, a minister (ordinary and extraordinary,) and have travelled with one for some weeks. I have dined with a *Chargé d'Affaires*, and lived with consuls, &c. I have visited and conversed with '*Red Jacket*,' the great Indian warrior: I have

* Brodie, p. 211, ed. 1851.

visited and been visited by a Bishop. I have frequently partook of the delicious Hungarian wine (*tokay*),—Prince Esterhazy's; as also of Prince Schwartzenburgh's old hock, said to have been 73 years old; and I was intimate with the brother-in-law of this last German nobleman. I have dined with a principal Hong merchant at Canton. I have sat next to the beautiful Madame Recamier, and Madame Carbanus, at the great dinner parties. I have written to the Prime Minister of England; and have received the late Earl of Liverpool's answer, with his thanks, &c. I was at Paris when the allies were met there. I have visited and breakfasted with the late Warren Hastings, Esq., at his seat in Gloucestershire. I have had permission with a party of friends to hunt over his grounds. Entertained, &c. two or three days at the sporting lodge of an Earl, now a Marquis. I have made a crimson silk net for a certain fashionable Marchioness, which she actually wore at her next great party of five or six hundred persons. I have danced with the Countess Bertrand, *i. e.* Mademoiselle Fanny Dillon, before she married the Marshal. I was at Napoleon's coronation. I have been invited to the Lord Mayor's and to the dinner of an Alderman of London."

Happily, the Hill dynasty was not destined to last long. He had given out, says Mr. Brodie, "that he was a very near relative of the Duke of Bedford, and that the Duchess seldom rode out in her carriage without him."* But whilst the people listened to his magnificent accounts of himself, and his noble friends, who should arrive on their shores, in H.M.S. *Actæon*, in 1837, but Captain Lord Edward Russell, a son of the Duke of Bedford!

A spectre could not have been a more appalling visitant to the so-called relative, who would have been forthwith taken from the place by Lord Edward Russell; but this could not have been done without orders. Soon afterwards, Captain H. W. Bruce, (now Admiral Bruce, Commander-in-chief on the coast of Africa,) arrived in H.M.S. *Imogene*, and carried off Mr. Hill, landing him in 1838 safe at Valparaiso.

Mr. Nobbs, during his absence from Pit-

* Brodie, p. 77.

cairn, was at the Gambier Islands, where he employed himself as a teacher, biding his time in patience, and employing, in his own homely and useful manner, the talent entrusted to him.

Gambier's group, about three hundred miles W.N.W. of Pitcairn, consists of eight islands, surrounded by coral reefs, inclosing a lagoon in which there are several secure anchoring places, but which contains dangerous knolls of coral. Captain Beechey gives a pleasing account of his visit to these islands in January 1826, and of his interviews with the natives. His vessel rode safely in the lagoon, where the crew caught a large quantity of fish. The people came out on rafts to the vessel, and were delighted with the presents which they received. One of them snatched up a small terrier dog, which was not intended for him; and it was only by force that he was prevented carrying it away. Others wanted to possess themselves, without a title, of a large Newfoundland dog; "but," says Captain Beechey, "he was big and surly enough to take care of himself."

In about nine months after Mr. Nobbs

had been at the Gambier Islands, the people of Pitcairn recalled him, with the other Europeans; the request for their return to the island being accompanied by an offer of payment of all their expenses; and they returned accordingly, without further delay.

Mr. Nobbs's active life in the Chilian service has been briefly noticed. In 1839, when engaged in the quiet, and sedentary, but scarcely less laborious duty of a pastor and teacher at Pitcairn, with his youthful pupils around him, he had the satisfaction of receiving, as a visiter to the island, General Friere, ex-president of Chili, who had known him eighteen years before. What a contrast to those former scenes, is afforded by the picture presented by the plain and simple words, found in the Island Register, respecting this visit!*

The following letter, signed by seven of the islanders, including the magistrate and the two councillors, will speak for itself. It is an answer to a communication received from the Rev. J. Moody, chaplain of H.M.S. *Thalia*, and since chaplain at the Falkland Islands:—

* See p. 250.

"Pitcairn's Island, South Pacific Ocean,
"July 20th, 1847.

"Reverend Sir,—We received, on the 26th of February last, by H.B.M.S. *Spy*, your acceptable present and truly valuable letter, which, so far from giving offence, is highly appreciated, and deposited in the archives of the island, to be referred to at public meetings and other suitable occasions. We extremely regret the circumstances which frustrated your intended visit, for we should be in the highest degree delighted to have made your acquaintance, received your advice, and, we trust, in some measure, your approbation; for we can assure you the report of our splitting into parties, &c. is incorrect. A few years since, a partially deranged impostor, named Joshua Hill, *alias* Lord Hill, came here, and made much disturbance; but he was removed by order of the British Government. Respecting the letter of which you saw a copy in the Oahu paper, so far from expressing the sentiments of the community, not more than three persons were acquainted with its contents. The rest of us were ignorant of its existence till we saw it published in the above-mentioned paper. That part of it reflecting on our respected and worthy pastor has been publicly retracted, and an apology sent down to the Sandwich Islands to be inserted in the same paper in which the letter referred to appeared. Public worship has never been discontinued, in fact, since the death of Mr. Adams, in 1829. We cannot call to mind six sabbaths in which divine worship, in accordance with the rules of the Established Church, has not been performed twice in the day. Whatever few exceptions there may have been, the cause was either the ill health of the teacher, or the unavoidable necessity of his attending on those who were very ill, or badly hurt. Moreover, we have a Bible class for the adults every Wednesday, and public school for the children five days a week. The number of children who attend school at present is fifty-three; they are all instructed, and make good progress. We have been thus explicit in the foregoing particulars, that you may understand the actual state of affairs among us. As British subjects, to honour and obey our most gracious sovereign, and all who are in authority under her, is our bounden duty, and we trust will ever be our privilege.

" And now, Reverend sir, we would bespeak your attention and interest for the following items :—The whole community are members of the Church of England, admitted thereto in their infancy by the rite of baptism; and the service of that Church is duly performed twice every Sabbath; but we are much in want of Prayer-books, Psalms, and Watts's Hymns for public use. The procuring some for us would be conferring a most essential service. Elementary books for the younger classes in the school, and Walkinghame's, or other books on arithmetic, for the more advanced scholars, are greatly needed. In short, the want of school requisites generally, impedes the progress of the rising generation.

" The next thing we would respectfully state our want of, is a medicine chest; for there is a vast amount of sickness among us, and serious accidents frequently occur. Our teacher possesses considerable skill as a physician, but his knowledge is often rendered comparatively valueless from the want of the necessary remedies.

"One thing more, before we conclude, we earnestly present to your consideration; and as it comes in an especial manner within the province of your holy office, we would indulge the hope that our application will be attended with success. The case in question is this: Our teacher, who has been with us for nineteen years in that capacity, and whose services to us are invaluable, has never received the licence or sanction of the proper authority in that Church of which we are a component part. This circumstance is a source of much anxiety, both to him and us, and as our number amounts to 138 (71 males and 67 females), and is rapidly increasing, we do most urgently, but most respectfully, solicit your application to the proper quarter for a pastoral letter, inducting or sanctioning our teacher into the holy office he has for so long a space of time unceasingly, untiringly, and worthily, filled on this island. That he is deserving such a mark of ecclesiastical approbation and favour, is justly and cheerfully acknowledged by the whole community; and of the great benefit which will accrue to us therefrom, no one can be more competent to judge than yourself.

"Hoping that this our public letter may obtain your favourable regard, we beg leave to subscribe ourselves,

"Your much obliged, very humble friends,

"CHARLES CHRISTIAN, *Magistrate.*
SIMON YOUNG, *Councillor.*
JOHN ADAMS, *Councillor.*
ISAAC CHRISTIAN.
FREDERICK YOUNG.
MAYHEW YOUNG.
ABRAHAM QUINTAL."

All these names will be recognised as those of descendants of the mutineers. Among them will be observed the name of John Adams. He is a grandson of the original John Adams, and is described by Mr. Nobbs, and other competent judges, as a young man of much talent and information.

The islanders also addressed a letter to Captain Charles Hope, who commanded the *Thalia* in the Pacific, in 1844, but who was prevented, much to his regret, from paying them a visit. He, however, sent them some useful presents. These did not reach them till February, 1847. In their letter of acknowledgment to Captain Hope, dated July 1847, is the following passage:—"Our number now amounts to one hundred and thirty-eight, and is rapidly increasing. Our teacher, who is a worthy man, and whose services are of great value to us, has never received the sanction or licence of the proper authorities in the Church to qualify him for the very important and prominent situation he fills. He is most anxious, and we are no less so, that he should be more formally inducted into the office of pastor; and for this purpose our humble request to you is, that you will (if it can be done with propriety) make our case known to the Bishop of London, or some other competent Dignitary, who would send a pastoral letter to our teacher, sanctioning and confirming him in the sacred office he for nineteen years has held among us."

Mr. Nobbs had been between eighteen and nineteen years in the midst of the people, when the above letters were written; and he had maintained and advanced among them, according to the teaching of the Church of

England, those good principles with which the very name of Pitcairn has been so long and so happily associated.

As their religion has been full of good fruits, so it has been of a quiet, sensible, and unostentatious kind. Inquiry having been made of Mr. Nobbs by some persons in the United States of America, a few years since, as to any instances of sudden and extraordinary conversion, which might have fallen under his notice, he replied, that his experience did not furnish any such cases from Pitcairn. In answer to the questions put to him, he remarked, in reference to the death-bed of Polly Adams, which will be found noticed in a subsequent page, as well as to some other instances:—

"Had inquiry been made for examples of HAPPY DEATHS, I could have replied with unmitigated satisfaction; for I have seen many depart this life, not only happy, but triumphant. And herein is, I think, the test of the Christian character; for when we see a person, who for a number of years has not only in word but in deed adorned the doctrine of God our Saviour in all things, brought by sickness or casualty to the confines of the eternal world, about to enter the precincts of the silent grave, yet with unabated energy and fervour proclaim his hope of a glorious resurrection; when we see a person suffering the most acute pain, exhorting and encouraging others to pursue the same path he has trod; telling the love of God to his soul, and of his desire to depart, that he may enter into the presence of his Redeemer; when we witness such unwavering confidence, amid such intense sufferings; and when the sanity of the patient is undoubted, can we hesitate to say at the demise of such an one, 'Let me die the death of the righteous, and let my last end be like his!' It has been my felicity to witness several departures of this description within a few years: two from accidents, one from a cancer in the breast, one shortly after child-birth, and one from disease of the heart. All these died in the faith. Some of the diseases were lingering, others rapidly fatal; but in all cases the subjects were 'strong in faith, giving glory to God.'"

It is pleasing to notice the terms of respect and regard in which the teacher is mentioned in the several communications from the island. Indeed, many valuable qualities appear to be united in him for the due discharge of his office. His good common sense, and plainness of speech, accompanied with an inoffensive firmness of conduct and manner, and that kind and Christian demeanour, without which all other important points of character in the "messenger of grace" are useless and unmeaning, distinguish him as the man for the situation to which it has pleased God to call him.

His remuneration had for many years been wholly inadequate to the necessities of his family, and to the maintenance of that respectable appearance which a person in such a position among the community ought to hold. For instance, in writing to a Clergyman at Valparaiso, in August 1844, Mr. Nobbs said,—

"My stock of clothing, which I brought from England is, as you may suppose, very nearly exhausted, and I have no friends there to whom I can with propriety apply for more. Until the last three years, it was my custom to wear a black coat on the Sabbath;

but since that period, I have been obliged to substitute a nankeen jacket, of my own making. My only remaining coat, which is quite threadbare, is reserved for marriages and burials; so that it is customary to say, when a wedding is going to take place, 'Teacher, you will have to put on your black coat next Sunday,' which is equivalent to informing me, that a couple are going to be married."

In 1849 Captain Fanshawe said: "Mr. Nobbs appears to be very much respected by all; and his virtuous demeanour, and careful education of the young, bear testimony to the faithfulness with which he has discharged his duty. The heads of families have obviated the necessity of his seeking elsewhere some more remunerative employment, by making over to him so much land as to place him, in that respect, on an equality with themselves."

It will gratify the reader to learn that this worthy and humble-minded Pastor has lately had a sufficient provision made for his comfort, and suitable appearance as a Clergyman.

The Rev. Wm. Armstrong, writing in 1849

respecting the islanders, reported, that they continued to receive much benefit from the services of Mr. Nobbs, "as their religious teacher, their schoolmaster, and their doctor." During an epidemic which prevailed in 1848, the attacks of which not more than twenty out of one hundred and fifty, escaped, Mr. Nobbs attended them from house to house, day and night, for a period of two months, with great success; only one, (an infant,) having died. It appeared that, on his proposing to accept a free passage to Valparaiso, that he might accompany thither his eldest son, Reuben, a great-grandson, on his mother's side, of Fletcher Christian, and then return to his people, the whole of his adopted countrymen came and begged that it might not be so, as they could not bear to part with him. This appeal prevailed; and, on Reuben's quitting the island for Valparaiso, to settle in the world, his father gave the whole of the money he possessed, amounting to eight dollars, to his son. All the families joined in fitting him out to the best of their power, furnishing him with a supply of clothes, and making up altogether a purse of more than forty dollars; several contributing every cent they had.

Mr. Nobbs received, with much delight, by Commander Dillon, of the *Cockatrice* schooner, in 1851, several gratifying letters from Mr. Armstrong, and Reuben. This young man, who was twenty-two years of age in September 1852, has acquired an excellent character, and earned the confidence of his employers, merchants at Valparaiso; but he is about to return to the island, in compliance with the wish of his mother, who has been very unhappy in consequence of his absence. He will therefore be conveyed in the *Portland* from Valparaiso to Pitcairn; and from the piety of his character, and general intelligence, there is good reason to hope that he will prove a valuable help to his father, and a blessing to his fellow-islanders.

The late excellent Captain Worth, of her Majesty's ship *Calypso*, who visited the island in 1848, afforded the following testimony to the amiable character and the happy state of the Pitcairn islanders:—

"We arrived here on the 9th March, (1848,) from Callao, but the weather being very bad, stormy and squally, as you know there is no landing except in a small nook called Bounty Bay, and very frequently not even there—indeed, never in ship's boats, from the violence of the surf—I did not communicate with the shore till the next day, when, having landed safely all the presents I brought for the inhabitants from Valparaiso, I landed myself with half the officers and youngsters, the ship standing off and on, there being no anchorage. I made the officers divide the day between them, one half on shore, the other on board; so they were gratified with visiting these interesting people. I never was so gratified by such a visit, and would rather have gone there than to any part of the world. I would write you a very long letter about them, but time presses; and I will only now say they are the most interesting, contented, moral, and happy people that can be conceived.

"Their delight at our arrival was beyond anything; the comfort, peace, strict morality, industry, and excessive cleanliness and neatness that was apparent about everything around them, was really such as I was not prepared to witness; their learning and attainments in general education and information really astonishing; all dressed in English style; the men a fine race, and the women and children very pretty, and their manner really of a superior order, ever smiling and joyous; but one mind and one wish seems to actuate them all. Crime appears to be unknown, and if there is really true happiness on earth, it surely is theirs.

"The island is romantic and beautiful; the soil of the richest description, yielding almost every tropical fruit and vegetable: in short, it is a little paradise. I examined their laws, added a few to them, assembled them all in the church, and addressed them, saying how gratified I was to find them in the happy state they were, advising them to follow in the steps of virtue and rectitude they had hitherto done, and they would never want the sympathies of their countrymen (*i. e.* English) who were most interested about them. I added such advice as I thought useful, and such suggestions as would, of course, be to their advantage. It was really affecting to see these primitive and excellent people, both old and young, 140 in the whole, looking up to me, and almost devouring all I said, with eager attention, and with scarcely a dry eye amongst them; and, 'albeit unused to the melting mood,' I found a moisture collecting in my own which I could scarcely restrain,—they were so grateful, so truly thankful, for all the kindnesses that had from time to time been shown them, and the interest in their welfare shown by us and our countrymen. I had all the men and most of the women on board; but there was such a sea on, that the poor girls were dreadfully sea-sick. I fired some guns and let off rockets on the night of our departure, and they returned the compliment by firing an old honeycombed gun belonging to the *Bounty*. I set them completely up—gave them 100lbs. of powder, ensign and union-jack, casks of salt beef and pork, implements of agriculture of all kinds, clothes, books, &c.; and sailed, on the evening of the 11th, for Tahiti."

Mr. Armstrong, in a letter, dated Valparaiso, Oct. 18, 1849, said:—

"The people tell me they have, for the

present, a good supply of books, having received a very suitable grant from the *Society for Promoting Christian Knowledge.* The whole of the books will, I am sure, highly delight them; and, from all I hear, I have no doubt they will be prized, and made good use of. You will be glad to learn that they are all well educated, the young men being instructed in navigation, and some of the lower branches of the mathematics; and that they live together in the greatest harmony, and in the strictest observance of religious duties, public, family, and private, with every appearance of perfect freedom from all crime, and bearing the stamp of extreme innocence and simplicity. A new regulation has been recently made for the distribution of all their books among the families, they having been before kept as public property, as it was believed that they would be more read and valued in that way, and for which purpose shelves have been put up in all their houses, which are very neat and comfortable, though more like ships' cabins than dwelling houses. The reason they give for this arrangement is, that they are in the habit of walking into each other's houses with the same freedom as into their own, and taking up a book, will sit down and read it aloud or not, as they feel disposed."

Mr. Armstrong had for some years shown a warm feeling of regard for the happiness and welfare of the islanders. He had not only been instrumental in transmitting some valuable presents by way of additions to their comforts, but had written them encouraging letters by H.M.S. *Basilisk*, Captain H. Hunt, which touched at the island in July 1844. He afterwards received the following pleasing letters from some of those whom he had delighted to benefit:—

"To the Rev. William Armstrong.

"Pitcairn's Island, Aug. 7, 1845.

"REV. SIR,—Please to receive our united thanks for the presents which you have sent us. We have prepared some native commodities for you, and would have sent them by this vessel, but the weather not being fine, and the captain being in great haste, it was delayed until another opportunity should present itself. The inhabitants are doing well; we have a good school, and religion is in a flourishing condition; and I trust by the grace of God it will continue to be so. God Almighty be with you, and bless you now and for ever. Amen.

"Yours,

"ARTHUR QUINTAL, JUN.

"Chief Magistrate.

"P.S.—We should like to hear from you by this same man, the name of the Admiral, his character, &c."

"Pitcairn's Island, South Pacific Ocean,
"Lat. 25° 4' S., Long. 130° 8' W.
"Sept. 26th, 1844.

"HONOURED SIR,—Please to accept my humble thanks for your condescension and kindness in administering to our necessities, and expressing such solicitude for our welfare. I hope myself and schoolfellows will ever retain sentiments of gratitude both toward you and our other friends in Valparaiso; and I humbly pray the God and Father of our Lord Jesus Christ will have you in his holy keeping, and that after this life I may be permitted to see you all, face to face, in the presence of Him who loved us, and washed us in his own blood. To Him be glory for ever and ever. Amen.

"LOUISA QUINTAL."

"Pitcairn's Island, South Pacific Ocean,
"Lat. 25° 4′ S., Long. 130° 8′ W.
"Sept. 26th, 1844.

"REVEREND AND HONOURED SIR,—Please to accept my humble thanks for the interest you are pleased to take in our welfare, and also for the presents you and our other friends in Valparaiso have sent us; and may they and you be rewarded a thousandfold both in a temporal and spiritual sense. And may the grace of our Lord Jesus Christ, and the love of God, and the fellowship of the Holy Ghost, be with you all. Amen.

"I am, Reverend Sir,
"Your grateful servant,
"MIRIAM CHRISTIAN."

From the Chief Magistrate of Pitcairn's Island to the Rev. Mr. Wm. Armstrong.

"Pitcairn's Island, April 6th, 1848.

"DEAR FRIEND,—Long have I heard of you, though not acquainted with you, but have often heard of your friendship towards us, Pitcairn Islanders. Now I have taken this opportunity to write these few lines to you, informing you of the state of things in our little island. We are all getting on very well. I hope that you and the rest of our friends are getting on well, as we are. I return you thanks for your kind letter, which I have received from H.M. ship *Calypso;* also the present which is sent by you and the rest of the kind gentlemen at Valparaiso. We have received from you all such things as are very valuable to us,—spades, saws, pots, and other articles. We have received them all with the greatest pleasure, and I return you all a thousand thanks for them. The presents are divided equally amongst us all, from the oldest woman to the youngest child; we are in number 141.

"Kind friend, this is the first opportunity I have had to write to you. I will thank you very much if you will take this fund of money which you will see in this paper, and buy me a few fish-hooks of the size you will see in the paper; and also for my family's use six copies of Watts's Hymn-books, and one Family Bible.

" Friend, I bid you farewell. Perhaps it may not be our chance to meet in this world, but I hope we may in a better world, where saints and angels meet; and if it be our good luck to meet there, there we shall meet to part no more. I am obliged to close my letter in great haste.

" I remain,

" Your sincere friend and well-wisher,

" George Adams,

" Chief Magistrate of Pitcairn's Island."

Besides these letters, now before the author, he has some neatly written "copies," in a small round hand, signed respectively by Albina M'Coy, Reuben Elias Nobbs, Miriam Christian, Robert Buffett, Jemima Young, Martha Young, James Chester Adams, John Adams, David Buffett, Simon Young, Frederic Young. The two latter are grandsons of Edward Young, who was a midshipman on board the *Bounty*, and one of the mutineers. These copies are from well-chosen originals, given by their master to his pupils as exercises in writing. The following are specimens :—

"*Religion conduces both to our present and future happiness.*

"*Wisdom and understanding should be treasured in your heart.*

"*Kingdoms and crowns must eventually be laid in the dust.*

"*Strive to deserve the friendship and approbation of good men.*"

There is also a leaf out of Martha Young's cyphering-book. She is now Mrs. David Buffett. The two pages are filled with accurately finished sums in the Rule of Three and Practice.

The School-house is a substantial building, about 56 feet long by 20 wide, conveniently supplied with forms, desks, slates, books, and maps. This room is fitted up and used for the performance of Divine Service on Sundays, and such other days as are appointed on the island. At one end there is a pulpit, and a small space allotted for the use of the pastor.

In a letter from some of the elder pupils to Captain Hope, in August 1847, an interesting report is given of the school-duties, and times of attendance :—

"We attend school five days in the week, five hours each day. Our routine of school-duties is as follows:—namely, Commence with prayer and praise; conclude with the same. Monday, recital of weekly tasks, reading the Holy Scriptures, writing, arithmetic, and class spelling. Tuesday, the same as on Monday. Wednesday, reading in history and geography, transcribing select portions of Scripture, &c. Thursday, similar to Monday and Tuesday. And on Friday, which is the busiest day of the week, transcribing words with their definitions from Walker's Dictionary; read hymns, or other devotional and moral poetry; repeat Watts's, and the Church Catechism; arithmetical tables, &c. &c.; and emulative spelling concludes the whole: we are generally an hour longer at school on this day than any other. On Wednesday afternoon the elder scholars attend the Bible class, with their parents. On the Sabbath, Divine Service is performed twice, and all who can possibly attend do so.

"The present so kindly sent us by the Rev. Mr. Thompson, received so much injury from wet before it reached us, as to be nearly useless. We regret this much, because we were greatly in need of school requisites generally. If the request is not improper, will you, honoured Sir, procure for us some copy-slips, or models for writing, and a few of Walkinghame's Arithmetic, with a Key to the same? for we often hear our Teacher say, if he had these helps, his work would be much easier; and we heartily wish he could obtain the means of making it so."

It is gratifying to learn that the school has been well attended to during the absence of the master. On this a few words will be added presently.

CHAPTER VII.

INVITATION TO ADMIRAL MORESBY—VISIT OF AN ENGLISH ADMIRAL TO THE ISLAND—HIS LETTERS AND THOSE OF HIS SECRETARY AND CHAPLAIN—ARRIVAL AT VALPARAISO —MR. NOBBS IN ENGLAND—HIS ORDINATION AS DEACON AND PRIEST — HIS INTERVIEW WITH THE QUEEN AND PRINCE ALBERT — RETURN HOMEWARD BY NAVY BAY AND THE ISTHMUS OF PANAMA — INTELLIGENCE FROM PITCAIRN—THE FIRST COMMUNION ON THE ISLAND.

THE narrative has now reached an important era in the annals of Pitcairn. The first arrival of an English Admiral at the island in August 1852, may be considered an historical event among the community there; and it may be reasonably hoped that the result of his visit will prove a blessing to the people.

Rear-Admiral Moresby, C.B., who had long been interested in the state and prospects of the islanders, received in July, 1851, the following warm and hearty invitation, signed by thirteen of the female inhabitants, in the name of all of their sex on the island :—

"Pitcairn, July 28th, 1851.

"HONOURABLE SIR,—From the kind interest you have evinced for our little community in the letter which you have sent our excellent and worthy Pastor, Mr. Nobbs, we are emboldened to send you the following request, which is that you will visit us before you leave this station; or if it is impossible for you to do so, certainly we, as loyal subjects of our gracious Queen, ought to be visited annually, if not more, by one of her ships of war.

"We have never had the pleasure of welcoming an English Admiral to our little Island, and we therefore earnestly solicit a visit from you. How inexpressibly happy shall we be if you should think fit to grant this our warmest wish. We trust that our very secluded and isolated position, and the very few visits we have of late had from British ships of war, will be sufficient apology for addressing the above request to you. With fervent prayers for your present and future happiness, and for that of our Queen, and Nation,

"We remain, Honoured Sir,

"Your sincere and affectionate well-wishers,

CAROLINE ADAMS, DORCAS YOUNG, SARAH M'COY, SARAH ADAMS, PHŒBE ADAMS, JEMIMA YOUNG, REBECCA CHRISTIAN, HANNAH YOUNG, NANCY QUINTAL, ELIZA QUINTAL, RUTH QUINTAL, RACHEL EVANS, SARAH NOBBS,	In the name, and on behalf, of all the rest of the female sex on the Island.

It will be seen from the subjoined narrative, that this invitation was accepted. The lively account, which has been supplied by Mr. Nobbs, of the reception of Admiral Moresby, will serve to place the reader in possession of many interesting facts connected with the present state of the island.

"On the 7th of August, 1852 (at noon),

a vessel was reported, which at sunset was strongly suspected of being a ship of war. The hours of the night passed tediously away, and before sunrise next morning several of our people were seated on the precipice in front of the town, anxiously waiting the report of a gun from the ship, which would give positive confirmation to the overnight suspicion of her being a ship of war; nor were they kept long in suspense: the booming of a cannon electrified the town, and the whole community were thrown into a state of intense excitement, more especially as it was quickly observed that she wore an Admiral's flag!

"Our boat repaired on board, and, after a short time, another from the ship was seen approaching the shore. The teacher and some others went to the landing-place, and had the honour and pleasure of welcoming to Pitcairn Rear-Admiral Moresby, Commander-in-Chief—the first officer of that rank that ever visited Pitcairn. The admiral received our greetings of welcome in a most urbane manner, and both himself and his secretary, Mr. Fortescue Moresby, were pleased to express themselves much gratified with all they saw and heard. The admiral attended divine service, and was evidently surprised at the improvement the people had made in singing by note; especially as their friend Carleton had so very limited a time for instructing them. In the afternoon the Rev. Mr. Holman read prayers, and preached a sermon, most appropriate to the occasion, from 1st Cor. 15th chap. last verse.

"The admiral, in the course of conversation, learned from the inhabitants that they had a great desire for the ordination of their pastor, in order that he might be qualified to administer the Sacrament of the Lord's Supper; and, with great kindness, proposed to send Mr. Nobbs to England for that purpose, leaving the Rev. Mr. Holman to officiate in his stead. The inhabitants did not accede to this most generous offer so readily as they ought to have done; and the reason they gave was, that in case of sickness they would have no one to prescribe for them. The admiral told them they might do as they liked, but they were certainly much wanting to themselves, and their children, if they let so favourable an opportunity pass without improving it. He explained to them, very clearly and forcibly, the necessity of an ordained clergyman being established among them, and the disabilities their children laboured under until such an event took place. They listened with breathless attention to the paternal advice of the admiral, and most readily acquiesced in all his expansive views of the subjects most vitally connected with their welfare. But still they evinced a backwardness in agreeing to part with their teacher. The admiral, on perceiving this, kindly told them he would give them till eleven o'clock to come to a decision, and that he would not retire till that period.

" During their debate one of them came to inquire of the admiral, whether Mr. Holman would teach the public school. The admiral replied, 'Certainly.' On this the man went away; and at eleven o'clock, as no answer had arrived, the admiral went to bed. About twelve o'clock word was brought, that the community had agreed to let their teacher go, which was duly reported next morning to the admiral, who remarked that they had done well in consenting to Mr. Nobbs's departure, and that he would take upon himself the responsibility of the expenses incurred necessarily by Mr. Nobbs, although he had no doubt there were friends of the Pitcairn Islanders who would cheerfully unite with him; and further, they would never lack friends so long as they continued to deserve them.

"As the point was now decided, Mr. Nobbs was requested to hold himself in readiness for embarkation, the admiral generously undertaking to supply him with articles in which his scanty wardrobe was deficient. On seeing the necessity there was of an educated female to improve the domestic habits of the women generally, and hearing Mr. Nobbs remark that he would send one of his daughters to Valparaiso for improvement, that she might on her return instruct the others, but that he could not command funds for doing so, the admiral replied,—'Take your child with you, and I will put her to school while you are gone to England; and when you come back you can take her to the island with you.'

"And now comes the leave-taking,—the

venerable and benevolent commander-in-chief of her Majesty's forces in the Pacific, standing on the rocky beach at Bounty Bay (the very spot where the mutineers had landed sixty-two years before), himself the oldest person there, by fifteen years, surrounded by stalwart men and matronly women, youths, maidens, and little children, every one in tears and most deeply affected, formed a truly impressive scene. The boat was some time in readiness before the admiral could avail himself of an opportunity to embark. Some held him by the hand, the elder women hanging on his neck, and the younger ones endeavouring to obtain a promise that he would revisit them. As a number of the men went on board with the admiral, a similar scene occurred there; and as the last boat pushed off from the ship, some of the hardy tars standing in the gangway were detected in hastily brushing away a tear. The frigate now stood in for the last time, and, hoisting the royal standard, fired a salute of twenty-one guns. The tars manned the rigging, and gave three hearty cheers, and one cheer more. The islanders responded:

the band struck up 'God save the Queen;' and the stately *Portland* started on her track. May He who stilleth the raging of the waves waft her propitiously to her destined port! To Admiral Moresby, Mr. Fortescue Moresby, Captain Chads, and the officers generally, the people of Pitcairn are much indebted for many, very many favours. That they will long be gratefully remembered, admits not of a doubt; and that the inhabitants may continue to conduct themselves as becomes people so highly favoured is most devoutly to be wished."

The following letter from Admiral Moresby to the Admiralty, will further illustrate the subject of Pitcairn, its people, and Pastor:—

"*Portland*, at sea, lat. 25° 25′ S., long. 126° 29′ W.
August 12, 1852.

"Sir,—Continuing the report of my proceedings from the 27th ult., as detailed in my letter No. 71, I request you will inform the Lords Commissioners of the Admiralty, that after passing over the position assigned to Incarnation Island without seeing it, we made Pitcairn's Island on the morning of the 7th instant.

"Early on Sunday, the 8th, I landed. From this time to the period of our departure, on the 11th, I remained on shore, and a constant intercourse was kept up with the *Portland.*

"It is impossible to do justice to the spirit of order and decency that animates the whole community, whose number amounts to 170, strictly brought up in the Protestant faith, according to the Established Church of England, by Mr. Nobbs, their pastor and surgeon, who has for twenty-four years zealously and successfully, by precept and example, raised them to a state of the highest moral conduct and feeling.

"Of fruits and edible roots they have at present abundance, which they exchange with the whalers for clothing, oil, medicine, and other necessaries; but the crops on the tillage ground begin to deteriorate, landslips occur with each succeeding storm, and the declivities of the hills, when denuded, are laid bare by the periodical rains. Their diet consists of yams, sweet potatoes, and bread-fruit; a small quantity of fish is occasionally caught; their pigs supply annually upon an average about 50 lbs. of meat to each individual; and they have a few goats and fowls. Their want of clothing and other absolute necessaries is very pressing, and I am satisfied that the time has arrived when preparation, at least, must be made for the future, seven or eight years being the utmost that can be looked forward to for a continuance of their present means of support. The summary of the year 1851 gives—births, 12; deaths, 2; marriages, 3. On their return from Otaheite they numbered about 60, of whom there were married 13 couple; the rest from the age of 16 to infancy.

"Mr. Nobbs was anxious to avail himself of my offer to convey him to Valparaiso, and thence enable him to proceed to England, for the purpose of obtaining ordination. At a general meeting of the inhabitants their consent was given, provided I would leave the chaplain of the *Portland* until Mr. Nobbs returned: the advantage is so obvious that I feel confident their lordships will approve my consenting. From the anxiety which has been expressed by high authorities of the Church for Mr. Nobbs's ordination, I anticipate that it will be effected with so little delay that he will be enabled to return to Valparaiso by the middle of January.

"I was unable to comply strictly with the list of articles which their lordships authorized me to give the islanders. I enclose a list of what we supplied; they were greatly wanted and gratefully received. The crew of the *Portland* also requested permission to give a portion of their allowance, and also that they might be allowed to send them a whale-boat, with other stores from Valparaiso.

"Captain Chads and the officers were most generous. I was fortunate in procuring at Borobora* a young bull and heifer, also a ram, accidents having befallen the ones previously sent. The packet of seeds forwarded in their lordships' letter, No. 132, of the 4th of December, 1851, was duly delivered.

"Should any unfortunate circumstance prevent the periodical visits of the whale-ships, they would be left entirely to the charitable consideration of her Majesty's Government. The crews of the whale-ships

* This is sometimes written, Bolabola.

have invariably conducted themselves with marked propriety. They take their turn of leave on shore, and their sick are received and nursed with the greatest care.

" The *Adeline Gibbs*, American whaler, Mr. Weeks, master, was there during our visit. Mr. and Mrs. Weeks were living ashore. It would be a happy circumstance if a person like her could be found to reside among them.

" I forward a continuation of their journal since that published by Mr. Brodie—a very correct statement, which renders unnecessary any further remarks.

" I have, &c.

" FAIRFAX MORESBY,

" Rear-Admiral, and Commander-in-Chief."

The Admiral also wrote thus from *The Portland*, at sea, August, 1852:—

" Of all the eventful periods which have chequered my life, none have surpassed in interest, and I trust in hope of future good, the last, our visit to Pitcairn; and surely the hand of God has been in all this, for by chances the most unexpected, and by favourable winds out of the usual course of the trades, we were carried in eleven days to Pitcairn's from Borobora. It is impossible to describe the charm that the society of the islanders throws around them under the providence of God. The hour and the occasion served, and I have brought away their pastor and teacher for the purpose of sending him to England to be ordained, and one of his daughters, who will be placed at the English clergyman's at Valparaiso, until her father's return. The islanders depend principally for their necessary supplies on the whaling ships, which are generally American. Greatly to their credit, the men behave in the most exemplary manner, very differently from what I expected. One rough seaman, whom I spoke to in praise of such conduct, said, 'Sir, I expect, if one of our fellows was to misbehave himself here, we should not leave him alive.' They are guileless and unsophisticated beyond description. The time had arrived when preparation for partial removal was necessary, and especially for the ordination of their pastor, or the appointment of a Clergyman of the Established Church.

"They are thoroughly versed in Bible history, which has hitherto kept them from listening to the advances of some over-heated imaginations. I stayed for days upon that speck in the ocean, but rising like a paradise from its bosom. I believe there was scarcely a dry eye in the ship when the islanders took their leave. We ran within hail of the settlement, hoisted the royal standard, fired a salute, and cheered them."

Extract from a Letter from the Admiral's Secretary.

"At 6. 30, A.M. of the 9th, as we were dancing along about eight knots an hour before a fresh breeze, we discovered a thin blue shadow, whose outline appeared to be too well defined to be a cloud: at 9 we were certain that we saw Pitcairn's Island. Having read so much of the mutiny of the *Bounty*, and the subsequent romantic history of the mutineers, which has resulted in the formation of a colony celebrated for their virtue, and simplicity, and religion, I experienced a feeling of something (I know not what to call it) on approaching the island, that I have felt when visiting some spot held sacred either from history or from being the scene of some Biblical relation; it is a secret kind of satisfaction. Having a fair wind, we hoped about noon to be on shore; but whilst we were yet twenty miles from the island, the wind came directly foul, and fell light, so that we hardly held our own, owing to the heavy swell, and all day we remained endeavouring to work up. What a little spot it appears on the vast Pacific! a mere rock, apparently incapable to resist the mighty waves of so vast an ocean. Easily indeed would a ship not knowing its exact position miss it. The mutineers might well deem themselves secure on so small an island, so remotely situated at that time. Also these seas were but little frequented; but even now, to give you an idea of their vast extent, notwithstanding the thousands of ships that are trading on them, we have only seen one ship at sea, and our track measures 4,500 miles. When we get close to the land, or some well-known port, we see a few. During the night we got a slant of wind, and at 6, Sunday morning the 8th, we were close to the island. The Admiral fired a gun to give notice of our arrival. A whale-boat full of the islanders soon came off, but before coming alongside they asked permission to come on board; then jumped up the side seven or eight fine, tall, robust fellows, and gave us a hearty shake-hands, and assured us of a hearty welcome when we went on shore.

"I was in my cabin with Philip M'Coy, one of the islanders, when the sentry came to tell me that it was prayer-time, for the admiral always has prayers before breakfast. I said to Philip, 'I shall be up again directly, if you will wait.' He paused a moment, and then said, 'May I come, sir?' 'Oh yes,' I answered. On going down, we met the rest of his companions, whom he told, and they all came in and knelt down to prayers. We then got a hurried breakfast, and the admiral and myself immediately landed in the cutter, the water being pretty smooth. This was the only time a ship's boat was able to land, for a heavy surf generally rolls in, breaking with terrific violence on the rocky shore. The proper way to land is to come to the back of the rollers in a ship's boat; a whale-boat then comes off, you get into her, and she immediately gets ready to obey the signal of a man who stands upon a rock on shore, and directly he waves his hat, the favourable moment has arrived, the men give way, and with wonderful rapidity the boat is borne on the top of the wave to the shore. They are very skilful, and in a heavy surf will generally land you dry.

"Mr. George Hunn Nobbs, their teacher or pastor, met us at the landing-place, and we at once ascended the cliffs by a steep winding path to a plantation of cocoa-trees, called the market-place, as all trade is carried on at this spot. Here the islanders met us and gave us a hearty welcome. Generally all the inhabitants assemble here to welcome the officers of a man-of-war; but as it was Sunday and early, they had not arrived. We continued our way by a pretty path winding through the trees to the town, meeting here and there detachments coming towards us. These all followed in our wake; and by the time we reached Mr. Nobbs's cottage, which is situated at the opposite end of the town, we had pretty well all the people after us.

"Never were seen so many happy smiling faces, all eager to look at the first admiral that ever came to their happy island; but not one tried to push his way, or make any attempt to get before another. If we said a kind word to any of them, they looked so happy and pleased! and we did not neglect to do so. There is not one in whose face good humour, virtue, amiability, and kindness does not beam, and consequently not one whose face is not pleasing.

"It was now church-time, and away we all went to Church. Mr. Nobbs officiated, and read the prayers impressively and earnestly: the most solemn attention was paid by all. They sang two hymns in most magnificent style; and really I have never heard any Church singing in any part of the world that could equal it, except at cathedrals; and the whole of the credit is due to a Mr. Carleton, who was left behind by accident from a whaler. (See 'Pitcairn's Island and the Islanders,' by Mr. Brodie.)

"Both sexes like to dress like English

people, if they can, on Sundays. The women complain that they cannot get shoes; but all the men can get them from the whalers. During the week, their dress consists chiefly of a dark-blue petticoat, and a white kind of shirt for the women; and for the men loose shirt and trowsers. Their food consists chiefly of yams, cocoa-nuts, bananas, tacco, oranges, &c. &c. a few fish; and in the yam season, each family kills a large pig, that during the hard work of digging yams they may have a little animal food. Sometimes they get goats'-flesh, and are trying to rear a few cattle they have there. The admiral gave them a young bull and cow, also a ram.

"Both sexes work very hard indeed. They usually rise at dawn, have family prayers, do the work that is necessary; about dusk have supper; then they go to the singing-school or to Mr. Nobbs, or meet to have a chat. About nine or ten, they go to bed, previously having family worship. Should one of the little ones go to bed or to sleep during his mother's absence, she immediately awakes it to say its prayers. Not a soul on the island would dream of commencing a meal or finishing without asking a blessing or returning thanks. Boys and girls can swim almost as soon as they can walk; consequently they can swim through the largest surf, and play about amongst the broken water on the rocks that we look at with terror. One of their greatest amusements is to have a slide, as they term it; that is, to take a piece of wood about three feet long, shaped like a canoe, with a small keel (called a surf-board); they then, holding this before them, dive under the first heavy sea, and come up the other side; they then swim out a little way until they see a rapid heavy sea come rolling in, the higher the better; they rest their breast upon the canoe or surf-board, and are carried along on the very apex of the surf at a prodigious rate right upon the rocks, where you think nothing can save them from being dashed to pieces, the surf seems so powerful; but in a moment they are on their legs, and prepared for another slide. Their method of fishing is equally dangerous; the women walk upon the rocks until they see a squid; then watching the retreating sea, they run in and try to pick the squid up before the advancing surf can wash them off; but frequently they are washed off, and then they have to exert all their skill to land, for they have no surf-board to help them.

"Christmas Day is a grand feast, and they keep it up in good style; but the Queen's birthday is their grand day; it is kept up with feasting and dancing (the only day they are allowed to dance on the island), and all sorts of merriment. Among the first questions everybody asks is, How is her Majesty the Queen?

"Away, away! we are off to the world again, truly sorry to leave this island; their happiness in this life consists wholly in virtue, and their virtue is their truest pleasure. They think that (and how really true it is!) the more religious and virtuous you become, the happier you are; deeming every sin to take from your enjoyment in this and the after life. If we were to take away the credit due to them of leading so good a life from principle, they would still continue, as they know that true pleasure is only to be obtained by obeying the will of God. Their temperance and industry give them health, food and cheerfulness; it gains for them universal esteem, respect, and sympathy; and as in this life they do not seek their pleasures in things below, but in a higher Power, so we may earnestly hope that the image of the Saviour will be found in their hearts, and in the next world that they may be peculiarly His own."

It will have been seen that the Rev. W. H. Holman was left at Pitcairn during the temporary withdrawal of Mr. Nobbs. The following is an extract from a letter of Mr. Holman's, to his father, Captain Holman, Teignmouth, Devon:—

"Pitcairn's Island, Sept. 5, 1852.

"And now as to my life on the island. I attend the school from a quarter past eight until twelve; dine at one; after dinner I accompany some one or other of the islanders to their work, and remain walking until sunset, when we return to supper. On Mondays, Wednesdays, and Fridays, after supper, I attend the singing-school, which is conducted on the Hullah system, and of which all the people are passionately fond. On other nights I have always visitors, who come to hear me talk of a world of which they know nothing beyond their own island.

"The accounts of the virtue and piety of these people are by no means exaggerated. I have no doubt they are the most religious and virtuous community in the world; and during the month I have been here, I have seen nothing approaching a quarrel, but perfect peace and good-will amongst all."

This part of the history cannot be concluded without an animated account by one of the voyagers, which brings the narrative down to Mr. Nobbs's arrival at Valparaiso, on his way to England:—

"He has officiated as minister during the last twenty-three years, greatly to the satisfaction of the islanders, if one may judge by the respect and affection which they entertain for him. We brought Mr. Nobbs as far as Valparaiso. More than one meeting was held by the elders, before they could bring themselves to consent to his leaving them, though only for a few months. At last their anxiety to have a regularly ordained clergyman prevailed. We found these excellent people fully deserving all the praise which has been bestowed upon them. They are like one large family, living in perfect harmony with each other. We were treated by them like brothers, and welcomed everywhere. The population is now twenty-one families. Arthur Quintal is the oldest man, and George Adams next, these being the only male survivors of the first generation. They are badly off for clothing, which they purchase from the whaling vessels occasionally touching there. Their money is derived from the sale of their surplus yams, &c.; but owing to the small size of the island, and the rapid increase of the population, they must, in a very few years, withhold from ships all supplies except water. The endeavours of Mr. Carleton and the Baron de Thierry to teach the natives singing, have been successful. They now sing together in parts beautifully, and are very grateful to those gentlemen for this tuition. They meet twice a-week to practise, and we heard them sing a variety of glees extremely well.

"We arrived on the morning of Sunday,

Aug. 8. As soon as we hove-to off Bounty Bay, Arthur Quintal, and George Adams, with as many as a whale-boat could contain, came on board to pay their respects to the first admiral who had ever visited them. Shortly after they requested leave to attend prayers in the admiral's cabin, which are read every morning by the chaplain. When breakfast was over, the band was ordered up, with which they were much delighted. They called first of all for 'God save the Queen,' Her Majesty having nowhere more loyal or affectionate subjects than the Pitcairn Islanders. Some marches, polkas, &c. called forth the remark, that such tunes seemed scarcely proper for Sundays.

"Our chaplain performed the afternoon service, and preached an excellent sermon. The hymns were sung in regular parts by the whole congregation. I doubt much whether any church in England, excepting cathedrals, can boast of such a good choir. The congregation were very nicely dressed; indeed, it is a great point to have white shirts on Sunday. The Sabbath is strictly observed. The crew of the *Portland* requested permission, which was granted, to present the islanders with three casks of rice, twelve bags of bread, and one cask of sugar; the value of these articles being charged against their wages. Mr. Nobbs left the shore amidst the tears and blessings of his little flock, by whom he is sincerely beloved.

"Before making sail on our course, we ran in close to the island, hoisted the royal standard at the particular request of the islanders, who had never before seen it displayed, fired a royal salute, manned the rigging, and gave three cheers for the islanders, which they answered heartily. We arrived at Valparaiso on the 30th August."

Mr. Nobbs having travelled by the Isthmus of Panama, arrived in England by the *Orinoco* steamer on Saturday, Oct. 16, 1852. Admiral Moresby had supplied him with the means of obtaining a passage from Valparaiso to London, and had offered 100*l.* towards such costs as might be incurred during his absence from the island.

On Mr. Nobbs presenting himself to the Bishop of London, his Lordship, in consideration of the high character given of him by Admiral Moresby, and other competent persons, acceded to his request to be admitted to holy orders.

On Sunday morning, October 24th, 1852, at an early service, an ordination took place at St. Mary's, Islington, under a special commission from the Bishop of London, by the Bishop of Sierra Leone, when Mr. Nobbs was admitted to Deacon's orders. Mr. Richard C. Paley, B. A. of St. Peter's College, Cambridge, a grandson of the celebrated Archdeacon Paley, was ordained at the same time; both candidates having been presented by the Rev. Henry Venn. Several of the clergy of the neighbourhood, and about twenty students of the Church Missionary College were present. Mr. Paley, who was a very young man, soon after entered upon his arduous and interesting Mission at Abbeokuta, Western Africa, but was stopped by the hand of death, almost at the commencement of his missionary career. The other candidate, more than twice his age, yet lives on, by God's good providence, for the benefit of his little flock in the Pacific.

On the 30th November following, St. Andrew's day, Mr. Nobbs was ordained Priest in Fulham Church, by the Bishop of London; his description in the letters of orders being "Chaplain of Pitcairn's Island." He was presented for priest's orders to the Bishop by the writer of this account.

During his two months' stay in England, Mr. Nobbs met with various marks of kindness. The prompt and courteous attention shown him at the Admiralty, by Mr. Stafford, Mr. T. T. Grant, and other gentlemen, he valued very highly. Among the visits which he paid, were those to the Duke and Duchess of Northumberland, the Bishops of London and Winchester, Archdeacon Grant, and Mrs. Heywood. Sir Robert H. Inglis received him as a welcome guest; and he was hospitably entertained at Killerton, Devon, by Sir Thos. Dyke Acland, one of the most cordial and serviceable of his many friends.

In consideration of the scanty resources of Pitcairn's Island, some noblemen and gentlemen were induced, on the recommendation of Admiral Moresby, with the kind aid of the Admiral's relatives in England, (Mrs.

Moresby, Mrs. Prevost, and Mr. and Mrs. R. A. White, of Grantham,) to raise a fund of moderate amount towards the passage and outfit of Mr. Nobbs, and for the supply of such things as were deemed requisite for the inhabitants. Labourers' and carpenters' tools, a proper bell for the Church, medicines, two or three clocks, clothing of various sorts, simple articles of furniture, and cooking utensils, were needed. Supplies of some of these things are likely to be required for a few years to come. It appears from recent accounts, that the crops on the island have lately failed, owing to a very long period of drought.

The *Society for Promoting Christian Knowledge*, at the General Meeting, held on the 7th of December, 1852, at which Mr. Nobbs was present, unanimously granted One Hundred Pounds towards the fund.

The *Society for the Propagation of the Gospel* placed Mr. Nobbs on its list of Missionaries, with a salary of 50*l.* per annum.

The Directors of the Royal Mail Steam Navigation Company generously provided him with a free passage to Navy Bay.

On Wednesday, December the 15th, two

days before he quitted England, Mr. Nobbs embarked at Portsmouth, on board the yacht *Fairy*, and proceeded, by appointment, to Osborne House, where he was received by Colonel the Hon. C. Grey, and, after a short time, was presented to Prince Albert. His Royal Highness was very kind, asked many questions as to the island, and appeared much pleased with the answers given. Mr. Nobbs having, towards the conclusion of this interview, humbly begged to be allowed to pay his duty in person to the Queen, and it having appeared, that Her Majesty had expressed her readiness to receive him, the Prince was pleased to present him to Her Majesty. His reception was highly gratifying to his feelings, as a dutiful subject, and the representative of the truly loyal community of Pitcairn. The Queen, who was most gracious and condescending in her demeanour towards him, was pleased to present him with her portrait. Portraits of Prince Albert, and the Royal Children, were added.

This highly-treasured gift was taken out in February, 1853, in Her Majesty's sloop, *Rattlesnake;* Captain Trollope, the com-

Q

mander, being instructed to leave it in the charge of the Commander-in-chief on the Pacific, for conveyance to Pitcairn.

Mr. Nobbs sailed from Southampton in the Royal Mail steam ship, *La Plata*, on the 17th December, 1852, and reached the island of St. Thomas early in the year 1853: from thence he proceeded in another steamer to Navy Bay. At the head of Navy Bay lies the town, which by the government of the Province, and in all official documents, is styled "Colon," but by the Americans, who are its founders and chief owners, is known by the name of "Aspinwall." There is the terminus of the railroad, by which the traveller is conveyed about 25 miles, at a high rate, to the station at Barbacoas, on the river Chagres. Thence there is a conveyance up the river by canoes, about 14 miles, to the town of Cruces. From Cruces the journey overland to Panama, about 25 miles, is completed on mules, over one of the very worst roads that exist in the known world. From the island of Tabôga, near Panama, an excellent steamer plies continually to Valparaiso, touching at Callao, the Port of Lima.

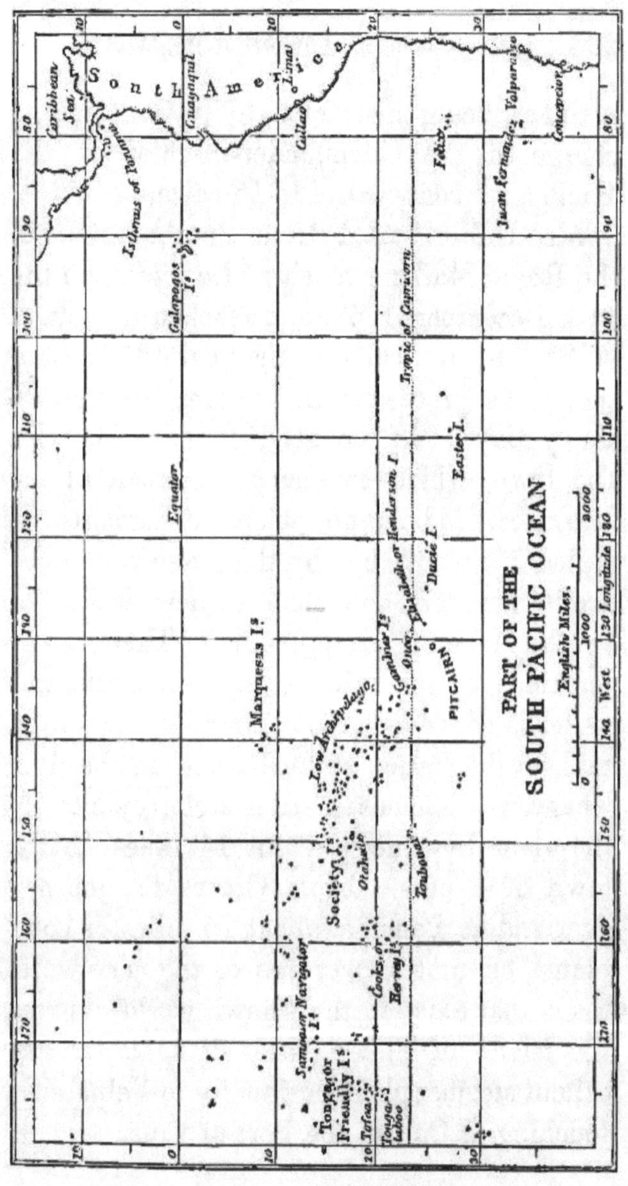
PART OF THE
SOUTH PACIFIC OCEAN
English Miles.
0
1000
2000
West
Longitude
Caribbean Sea
Isthmus of Panama
South America
Guayaquil
Lima
Callao
Equator
Galapagos Is
Marquesas Is
Low Archipelago
Society Is
Otaheite
Samoa or Navigator Is
Tonga or Friendly Is
Tofoa
Tonga taboo
Cooks or Hervey Is
Toubouai
Gambier Is
Oneo
Elizabeth or Henderson I
Ducie I.
PITCAIRN
Easter I.
Tropic of Capricorn
Felix
Juan Fernandez
Valparaiso
Concepcion

It will be interesting to many readers to learn, that the late admirable Bishop of Sydney, Dr. W. G. Broughton, recently travelled by this line, crossing the Isthmus of Panama, on his way from Lima to this country. His Lordship reached England on the 18th of November, 1852, the day of the funeral of his patron, the Duke of Wellington, and died in London, deeply and deservedly lamented, on the 20th February, 1853. He had expressed, in a letter to the author, much sympathy with the Pitcairn islanders, and their Pastor.

Mr. Nobbs, though a well-tried traveller, equal to the endurance of no small amount of hardship, experienced a full share of the trouble and annoyance for which the journey over the Isthmus of Panama is proverbial. He had purposely avoided taking much luggage. Not only, however, was the charge for conveyance exorbitant; but, notwithstanding all his care, he, for some time, lost sight of a trunk, which contained, among other articles of importance, a beautiful set of communion plate, which had been entrusted to his care by a friend at Fulham, for use in the church at Pitcairn. This painful event, added to the ill effect of the climate, brought on an attack of fever, the symptoms of which were slight, until his leaving Panama. By God's blessing this sickness passed away. Through the active zeal of Mr. Perry, the British Consul at Panama, the goods, which had been missing for a week, were safe in Mr. Nobbs's hands when he wrote. He had arrived at Valparaiso just too late for a vessel which had left for Pitcairn; and he had found his son and daughter in good health. Writing to the author from Valparaiso, he said:—

"After some detention and sickness, I was graciously permitted to arrive here on the 12th of February, and I am still detained waiting for the *Portland*. Oh, how I wish to be at home! The Admiral is in tolerable health, and so is the Reverend Mr. Hill, who, I believe, corresponds with you. I have divided the duty with him at the church on shore, ever since I have been here, besides the service on board one of the British ships of war, once on each Sabbath; so you see I am not idle. The agent for British steamers in these parts presented me with a free passage from Panama to Valparaiso, in the name of his Company, whose directors reside in Liverpool. I wish you, my friend, or our good Sir Thomas, would thank them for their kindness. I also intend doing the same. If you have anything to send to your correspondents in these parts, let it come round Cape Horn; for if it comes across the Isthmus of Panama, the charges will be enormous. Please to offer my grateful remembrances to all and every one to whom you think it right they should be offered, especially those kind and worthy brethren who attend your Society, and who have expressed so much interest in me and mine. So much for business, &c."

The distance from England to Pitcairn, by the route described, is about 10,160 miles.

In the first edition of this little book was the following passage :—

"From Valparaiso, should all go on prosperously with Mr. Nobbs, Admiral Moresby will convey him to Pitcairn in the *Portland;* and the islanders will probably welcome him home before the end of March. May it please God to guide him, in health and safety, to his distant flock! Who can adequately imagine the scene which will be presented on his landing among his friends on the island, to be parted from them no more on this side the grave?"

It appears from letters since received, that it would be near the middle of May before the pastor would be able to see his friends at Pitcairn again. In his last letter to the author, he said, "I hope my next will be dated Pitcairn's Island." Looking forward to the pleasure of being once more at home, he added, "Oh! that will be joyful." Whilst staying at Valparaiso, he will have heard the interesting intelligence respecting the islanders, which is conveyed by the Rev. W. H. Holman, in a letter forwarded by Admiral Moresby. The following is an extract from Admiral Moresby's letter to the author, dated Valparaiso, 31st January, 1853:—

"Truly my heart rejoices at the completion

of my wishes in Mr. Nobbs's ordination, and the future prospect opening to the Pitcairn community. A small sum will suffice to keep up a knowledge of the Tahitian language—the voice by which the extension of the Gospel will be forwarded. It fortunately happens that I have received this morning a letter from the Rev. W. Holman, dated Pitcairn, 21st December. I send a copy.

"I have now only to hope and trust, that it will please God to give his blessing to all that has been done."

Mr. Holman's letter to the Admiral, especially on the subject of the first communion on the island, speaks volumes in favour, not only of the people, but of the care and faithfulness of the pastor who had so long laboured to train them to all that is good:—

"Pitcairn's Island, Dec. 21st, 1852.

"The arrival of the English whaler, *Mary Nichols*, and her departure to-day for the Island of Chiloe, affords me an opportunity of communicating intelligence from this place. The *Cockatrice* arrived on the 17th of November, and left again on the 24th. The people are greatly pleased with the presents brought by her, and feel very grateful for the kindness of their friends. Two deaths have occurred since I last wrote, that of Mary Christian, on the 24th October, and a little boy, William Quintal, on the 1st of November, the latter from locked-jaw, occasioned by a thorn running into his foot. The assistant surgeon of the *Cockatrice* informed me, that no medical aid could have saved either case. The people are now quite healthy, with the exception of the slight indisposition caused by vaccination, which is proceeding very favourably, and which, I hope, will have succeeded in every case before your return.

"I am happy in being able again to report favourably of the high moral and religious character of the people. The latter has, I trust, been greatly improved by the serious and solemn thoughts occasioned by the first administration of the Holy Communion. The whole of the adult congregation (sixty-two) communicated."

CHAPTER VIII.

SOME ACCOUNT OF THE LAWS OF PITCAIRN—THE ISLAND REGISTER—LIST OF VESSELS MENTIONED IN THIS WORK WHICH HAVE TOUCHED AT THE ISLAND—MELANCHOLY ACCIDENT ON THE ISLAND.

SOME account will be expected of the Laws and Regulations of Pitcairn's Island.

LAW RESPECTING THE MAGISTRATE.

"The Magistrate is to convene the public on occasions of complaints being made to him; and on hearing both sides of the question, commit it to a jury. He is to see all fines levied, and all public works executed; and every one must treat him with respect. He is not to assume any power or authority on his own responsibility, or without the consent of the majority of the people. A public journal shall be kept by the magistrate, and shall from time to time be read; so that no one shall plead ignorance of the law for any crime he may commit. This journal shall be submitted to the inspection of those captains of British men-of-war, which occasionally touch at the Island.

"N.B. Every person, from the age of fifteen and upwards, shall pay a fine similar to masters of families.

LAWS REGARDING THE SCHOOL.

"There must be a school kept, to which all parents shall be obliged to send their children, who must previously be able to repeat the alphabet, and be of the age of from six to sixteen. Mr. Nobbs shall be placed at the head of the school, assisted by such persons as shall be named by the chief magistrate. The school-hours shall be from seven o'clock in the morning, until noon, on all days, excepting Saturdays and Sundays; casualties and sickness excepted. One shilling, or an equivalent, as marked below, shall be paid for each child per month, by the parents, whether the child attend school or not. In case Mr. Nobbs does not attend, the assistant appointed by the chief magistrate shall receive the salary in proportion to the time Mr. Nobbs is absent.

" Equivalent for money :—

	s.	d.
One barrel of yams, valued at	8	0
One barrel of sweet potatoes	8	0
One barrel of Irish potatoes	12	0
Three good bunches of plantains	4	0
One day's labour	2	0

The chief magistrate is to see the labour well performed; and goods which may be given for money, shall be delivered, either at the market-place or at the house of Mr. Nobbs, as he may direct."

It may here be remarked that the worthy schoolmaster, having become Godfather to many of the children, charges nothing for the instruction of these scholars.

LAWS RESPECTING LANDMARKS.

" On the 1st of January, after the magistrate is elected, he shall assemble all those who should be deemed necessary; and with them he is to visit all landmarks that are upon the island, and replace those that are lost. Should anything occur to prevent its accomplishment in the time specified (the 1st of January), the magistrate is bound to see it done the first opportunity.

LAWS FOR TRADING WITH SHIPS.

"No person or persons shall be allowed to get spirits of any sort, from any vessel, or sell it to strangers, or any person upon the island. Any one found guilty of so doing shall be punished by fine, or such other punishment as a jury shall determine on. No intoxicating liquor whatever shall be allowed to be taken on shore, unless it be for medicinal purposes. Any person found guilty of transgressing this law shall be severely punished by a jury. No females are allowed to go on board a foreign vessel of any size or description, without the permission of the magistrate; and in case the magistrate does not go on board himself, he is to appoint four men to look after the females.

LAWS FOR THE PUBLIC ANVIL, ETC.

"Any person taking the public anvil and public sledge-hammer from the blacksmith's shop, is to take it back after he has done with it; and in case the anvil and sledge-hammer should get lost by his neglecting to take it back, he is to get another anvil and sledge-hammer, and pay a fine of four shillings."

With regard to the laws as to CATS, FOWLS, &c., the Rev. G. H. Nobbs stated as follows:—

If a CAT is killed without being positively detected in killing fowls, however strong the suspicion may be, the person killing such cat is obliged, as a penalty, to destroy 300 rats, whose tails must be submitted for the inspection of the magistrate, by way of proof that the penalty has been paid.

If a FOWL is found destroying the yams or potatoes, the owner of the plantation, after giving due warning, may shoot the fowl, and retain it for his use, and may demand of the owner of such fowl the amount of powder and shot so expended, as well as the fowl. The fowls are all toe-marked.

GOATS, and other quadrupeds, are ear-marked.

If a PIG gets loose from its sty and commits any depredation, the owner is obliged to make good the damage, according to the decision of the magistrate, whose duty it is to survey the injury alleged to be done, and from whose decision a reference, if necessary, may be made to a jury; but the final appeal is to the captain of the next man-of-war touching at the island.

A Bank was set on foot a few years since at Pitcairn. The dollars, which were not very numerous, were allowed to accumulate for a time, partly with the object of purchasing a vessel. But the plan did not answer; and the several deposits were returned.

The Register of Pitcairn's Island, from 1790 to 1850, is a very interesting document, and will probably be of unspeakable value hereafter, as a record of names and events connected with that little world. A few extracts will be given.

The first entry occurs January 23d, 1790: "H.M.S. *Bounty* burned. Fasto, wife of John Williams, died. October Thursday Christian born."

The annals of 1793 are of a most melancholy kind, recounting the massacre of Fletcher Christian, John Mills, William Brown, John Williams, Isaac Martin; and the death of all the Otaheitan men, "part by jealousy among themselves, and others by the remaining Englishmen."

In 1794 we read of "a great desire in many of the women to leave the island: and of a boat built on purpose to remove them, launched, and upset." In August, the same year, "a grave was dug, and the bones of all the white men that had been murdered were buried." In November, "a conspiracy of the women to kill all the white men, when asleep in their beds, was discovered. They were all seized, a disclosure ensued, and all were pardoned." Nov. 30th, "the women attacked the white men, but no one was hurt. They were once more pardoned, and threatened the next time with death."

"1795, *May 6th.*—The first two canoes, for the purpose of catching fish, were made. Saw a vessel close in with the island. Mutineers much alarmed. Vessel stood out to sea Dec. 27th.

"1797.—Endeavoured to procure a quantity of meat for salting, and to make syrup from the ti-plant and sugar-cane.

"1799.—Matthew Quintal, having threatened to take the lives of Young and Adams, these two considered their lives in danger, and thought they were justified in taking away the life of Quintal, which they did with an axe.

"1800.—Edward Young, a mutineer, died of asthma.

"1817.—Arrived, ship *Sultan*, of Boston, Captain Reynolds; Jenny, a Tahitian woman, left here in the *Sultan*.

"1823.—Arrived, ship *Cyrus*, of London, Captain Hall; John Buffett came on shore, as schoolmaster, and John Evans also came on shore.

"1825, *Dec. 5th.*—Arrived, H.M.S. *Blossom*, Captain F. W. Beechey.

"1826, *Dec.* 19.—Jane Quintal left the island in the *Lovely*, of London, Captain Blythe.

"1828, *Nov.* 15*th.*—George Nobbs came on shore, to reside.

"1829, *March 5th.*—

John Adams died, aged 65.

JOHN ADAMS'S GRAVE, PITCAIRN.

"1830, *March* 15*th*.—Arrived, H.M.S. *Seringapatam*, Captain Hon. W. Waldegrave, with a present of clothes and agricultural implements and tools from the British Government.

"1831, *Feb.* 28*th*.—Arrived, H.M. Sloop *Comet*, Alexander A. Sandilands, and barque *Lucy Anne*, of Sydney, government vessel, J. Currey, master, for the purpose of removing the inhabitants of Pitcairn's Island to Tahiti.

"*March* 6*th*.—All the inhabitants embarked and sailed for Tahiti.

"*March* 21*st*.—Soon after our arrival at Tahiti, the Pitcairn people were taken sick.

"1831.—John Buffett and family, Robert Young, Joseph Christian, &c. sailed from Tahiti, in a small schooner; but, owing to contrary winds, they landed at Lord Hood's Island.

"*June* 21*st*.—John Buffett, and the others on Lord Hood's Island, embarked in the French frigate *Bordeaux Packet*, and on the 27th landed at Pitcairn's Island. During our absence our hogs have gone wild, and destroyed our crops. After we returned,

R

we employed ourselves in destroying the hogs.

"1838, *Nov.* 29*th.*—Arrived, H.M.S. *Fly*, Captain Russell Elliott, with a present from Rev. Mr. Rowlandson and congregation at Valparaiso. Captain Elliott proposed electing a chief magistrate, which was adopted; and Edward Quintal was chosen.

"This island was taken possession of by Captain Elliott, on behalf of the Crown of Great Britain, on the 29th of November, 1838.

"1839, *Nov.* 9*th.*—Arrived, H.M.S. *Sparrowhawk*, Captain J. Shepherd. The captain, several officers, and General Friere, ex-President of Chili, landed. In the afternoon the school-children were examined, and received the approbation of our respected visitors. Captain Shepherd afterwards divided some valuable presents among them.

"10*th.*—Captain Shepherd and his officers attended Divine service twice. At 5 P.M. they went on board. They sailed on the 12th.

"1840, *Feb.* 8*th.*—Mrs. Nobbs received a severe contusion on the shoulder, by the falling of a cocoa-nut from the tree.

"*Feb.* 13*th.*—Moses Young fell from a

cocoa-nut-tree, at least forty feet high, and was but slightly injured.

"1841, *Aug.* 18*th.* — Arrived, H. M. S. *Curaçoa*, Captain Jenkin Jones; and a most opportune arrival it was, for there were at least twenty cases of influenza among us." The Register goes on to describe the valuable services rendered by Captain Jones and the surgeon of the ship, Dr. Gunn. The *Curaçoa* sailed on the 20th.

"*Sept.* 19*th.*—Died, Isabella, a native of Tahiti, relict of Fletcher Christian, of the *Bounty*. Her age was not known; but she frequently said she remembered Captain Cook arriving at Tahiti.

"1843, *March* 4*th.*—Eleven of the inhabitants sailed in the barque *America*, for the purpose of exploring Elizabeth Island.

"5*th.*—Arrived, H.M.S. *Talbot*, Captain Sir T. Thompson, Bart. After remaining on shore, and adjusting some of the most pressing judicial cases presented to him, he went on board, and sailed for Valparaiso.

"11*th.*—Barque *America* returned from Elizabeth Island, our people bringing a very unfavourable report of it.

"1844, *July* 28*th*. — Arrived, H.M.S. *Basilisk*, Captain Henry Hunt, bringing presents from the British Government, Admiral Thomas, the Rev. Mr. Armstrong, &c.

"1845, *Jan.* 19*th*.—During the last week we have been employed in fishing up two of the *Bounty's* large guns. For fifty-five years they have been deposited at the bottom of the sea, on a bed of coral, guiltless of blood during the time so many thousands of mankind became, in Europe, food for cannon. But on Saturday last, one of the guns resumed its natural vocation—at least the innoxious portion of it—to wit, pouring forth fire and smoke, and causing the island to reverberate with its bellowing; the other gun is condemned to silence, having been spiked by some one in the *Bounty*.

"1845, *April* 16*th*."—The diary of this date contains a striking description of a storm, which, bursting over the island, greatly alarmed the inhabitants. A considerable portion of the earth was detached from the side of the hill situate at the head of a ravine, and carried into the sea; about 300 cocoa-nut-trees were torn up by the roots, and borne along with it; a yam-ground, containing 1,000 yams, totally disappeared; several fishing-boats were destroyed, and large pieces of rock were found blocking up the harbour in several parts. In the interior, all the plantain patches were levelled, and about 4,000 plantain-trees destroyed, one-half in full bearing, the other designed for the year 1846. "So that," says the annalist, "this very valuable article of food we shall be without for a long time. The fact is, that from this date until August, we shall be pinched for food. But God tempers the wind to the shorn lamb; and we humbly trust that the late monitions of Providence, namely, drought, sickness, and storm, which severally have afflicted us this year, may be sanctified to us, and be the means of bringing us, one and all, into a closer communion with our God. May we remember the rod, and who hath appointed it. May we flee to the cross of Christ for safety and succour in every time of need, always bearing in mind that our heavenly Father doth not willingly afflict the children of men."

The details which follow, respecting a

serious accident to the pastor's eldest son, Reuben E. Nobbs, which resulted in what appears to be confirmed lameness, are so characteristic of the kind and brotherly feeling subsisting in the island, that they must be quoted in full.

"1847, *Feb. 20th.*—This afternoon, as Reuben Nobbs was out in the mountain, shooting goats, his foot slipped, and he let fall his musket, which exploded and wounded him severely. The ball entered a little below the hip joint, and passing downwards, came through on the inside of the thigh, about half-way between the groin and the knee. Providentially, some persons were within call, who immediately ran to his assistance, and tore up their shirts to stanch the blood, which was pouring forth profusely. A lad was despatched to the village with the melancholy news; and in a few minutes the whole of the inhabitants capable of going were on their way to afford relief, headed by his affectionate mother, who was almost frantic with grief. In about an hour they returned, bearing him in a canoe, which they had taken up for that purpose. After some difficulty the blood was stanched, and the lad suffered but little pain. Every person was anxious to render assistance; the greater part of the male inhabitants remained at night, to be ready at a moment's warning to do anything that might be required. Towards midnight he fell asleep; and so ends this melancholy day.

"21*st.*—About daylight the wounded lad awoke, very much refreshed; he does not complain much, and has but little fever. The men and grown lads have formed themselves into three watches, to attend his wants, both day and night. It is most gratifying to his parents to see the esteem in which their son is held.

"22*d.*—Reuben Nobbs is free from pain, but there is a considerable accession of fever; it does not appear that either the thigh or hip-bone is injured, as he can move his leg without much difficulty or pain. From the great length of the internal wound, it is difficult to ascertain whether any of the wadding remains where the ball must have passed through.

"26*th.*—This morning a ship was reported; everybody appeared rejoiced, hoping to get some necessaries for their wounded friend.

On nearing the island, she proved to be H.M.S. *Spy*, Captain Wooldridge. 'Thank God!' was the grateful exclamation of many, on hearing it was a ship of war, on account of her having a surgeon on board. At 1 P.M. Captain Wooldridge and the surgeon (Dr. Bowden) landed, who immediately visited young Nobbs; and after probing the wound, and ascertaining the extent of the injury, gave his opinion that there was not much danger, and that with proper attention he would, in all probability, recover, although a narrower escape from death never came beneath his notice. Captain Wooldridge, being much pressed for time, informed the inhabitants he must sail that evening. After kindly interesting himself in the welfare of the island, and noting down such things as the community were most in want of, at sunset the *Spy* sailed for Valparaiso. Mr. and Mrs. Nobbs here take the opportunity of publicly recording their grateful acknowledgments to Captain Wooldridge and Dr. Bowden for the favours conferred on their son.

" *June 4th.*—Experienced a heavy gale from the westward, which, if it had been of long duration, would have done incalculable damage. A large piece of the banyan-tree was blown down, and the flagstaff broken in two pieces.

" 1848, *March* 9*th.*—Arrived H.M.S. *Calypso*, Captain H. Worth.

" 10*th.*—At 9 A.M. Captain Worth, and a party of officers, landed; and the greeting on both sides was most cordial. Our people, men, women, and children, are almost beside themselves."

Many valuable and useful presents were brought to the island. The next day the ship was discovered four miles from the land. Captain Worth, Dr. Domet, and others, again landed. The Doctor wishing to inspect the hieroglyphics, carved by the aborigines, went down the face of the cliff without the assistance of a rope—a most hazardous feat. It is stated that he was the first European who had performed it.

" At sunset the *Calypso* sailed, carrying with her our grateful aspirations, &c.

" 1849, *July* 10*th.*"—A very animated description is given, under this date, of the arrival of " the *Pandora*, Captain Wood, from

Oahu and Tahiti, bringing us Mr. Buffett back, who left us for the Sandwich Islands last summer.

"*July* 11*th*.—This evening Captain Wood left us, to our great regret; for though our acquaintance was but of two days' duration, the urbanity of Captain Wood, and his solicitude for our welfare, have made a deep and, we hope, a lasting impression on our hearts. That the good ship, *Pandora*, and all her gallant crew, may escape the perils of the deep, and before many months have elapsed, show her number some early day at Spithead, is the wish of their friends residing on the rock of the West.

"*Aug.* 9*th*.—The inhabitants are slowly recovering from the epidemic which has pervaded the island during the last month. So general was the attack, that the public school has been discontinued, and public service but once performed on each Sabbath, in consequence; the teacher being fully employed attending the sick.

"11*th*.—Arrived, H.M.S. *Daphne*, Captain Fanshawe, from Valparaiso, *viâ* Callao, bringing the *desiderata* of the community, viz. a bull, cow, and some rabbits. They were landed without any difficulty by our own boats. We also received from the Rev. Mr. Armstrong several boxes of acceptable articles, and a large case of books from the *Society for Promoting Christian Knowledge.* At 3 P.M. Captain Fanshawe and a party of the officers landed. At sunset they returned on board again, except the surgeon, who remained on shore, at the particular request of Mr. Nobbs, who required some advice about the sick.

" 12*th.*—At 1 P.M. Captain Fanshawe returned on shore, with a fresh party of officers, and attended divine service. Much persuasion was used by our young people to induce Captain F. to remain another day, but he told them he could not do so with propriety. At sunset they all returned on board, and H.M.S. *Daphne* sailed for Tahiti. Captain F. (as well as his officers) treated those of our people who went on board most kindly, and made most minute inquiries into our wants and actual condition. They were pleased to express their satisfaction at what they saw and heard, and left us deeply impressed with their courtesy and urbanity. May Almighty God have them in his holy keeping!

" *Sept.* 6*th.*—A large hair seal captured on the west side of the island. Fletcher Christian first discovered it among the rocks, and was much alarmed at the sight of it. He feared to go near it, lest it should be a ghost, (of which he has a great horror,) or some beast of prey, but quickly ascended the hill which overlooks the town, and gave the alarm. Some persons went over to his assistance, and shot the animal just as it was making its retreat into the sea.

" 20*th.*—This day was set apart as a day of fasting and prayer. Public service commenced at 11 A.M. and ended at 1 P.M. All who could get to Church attended. Text, Romans ii. 4, 5. One of the females fainted during service."

" SUMMARY.

" This year is unprecedented in the annals of Pitcairn's Island. We have been visited by two British men-of-war, the *Pandora*,

Captain Wood, and the *Daphne*, Captain Fanshawe. The commanders of these ships, and their officers, treated the inhabitants with the greatest kindness, and were pleased to express their entire approval of all they saw and heard. The *Daphne* brought us a bull and cow, and some rabbits, with a variety of other articles, from the Rev. Mr. Armstrong and other friends in Valparaiso. The cattle and the rabbits produced a great sensation. Another (to us) wonderful occurrence is the arrival of so many other ships under English colours, viz. eight from the Australian colonies, bound for California, and one whaling vessel from London; in all, nine merchantmen and two ships of war. American ships have dwindled down to six whalers and one from California; in her, Reuben E. Nobbs embarked for Valparaiso.

"George Adams saved the life of a child alongside of a ship in the offing.

"The inhabitants, with scarcely one exception, have suffered from sickness very severely during the months of August, September, and October. The school was discontinued, the children being too sick to attend, and the teacher was fully (and, thank God! efficiently) employed in ministering from house to house. Some of the cases were quite alarming, and the disease (the influenza) in general was more severe, but considerably modified from that of former years; violent spasms in the stomach and epigastric region were frequent in all stages of the complaint. At the close of the year, the inhabitants are enjoying much better health. May the recent affliction teach us so to number our days, that we may apply our hearts unto wisdom!

"1850, *Jan. 23d.*—This day was observed as the anniversary of the settlement of this colony, sixty years since. One survivor of that strange event, and sanguinary result, witnessed its celebration.* At daylight one of the *Bounty's* guns was discharged, and awakened the sleeping echoes, and the more drowsy of its inhabitants. At 10 A.M. divine service was performed. After the service, various letters received from the British Government and principal friends were read, and commented upon. At twelve o'clock

* Susannah, who died on the 15th of July following.

(noon), a number of musketeers assembled under the flagstaff, and fired a volley in honour of the day. After dinner, males and females assembled in front of the church (where the British flag was flying), and gave three cheers for Queen Victoria, three for the government at home, three for the magistrate here, three for absent friends, three for the ladies, and three for the community in general, amid the firing of muskets and ringing of the bell. At sunset, the gun of the *Bounty* was again fired, and the day closed in harmony and peace, both towards God and man. It is voted that an annual celebration be observed."

The following CONTINUATION OF THE REGISTER OF PITCAIRN'S ISLAND, taken up from the date of that published in the work of Mr. Walter Brodie, was placed in the hands of the author by the Rev. G. H. Nobbs.

"1850, *March 24th.*—Daniel McCoy and Lydia Young married.

"*April 20th.*—Charles Carleton Vieder Young born.

"*June 3d.*—John Pitcairns Elford (native of Adelaide, New South Wales) baptized.

15*th.*—Julia Christian died of dysentery.

" *July* 15*th.*—Susannah (a native of Tahiti, and last survivor of the *Bounty*) died from the prevailing epidemic and the exhaustion of old age combined.

" *Sept.* 18*th.*—Robert Charles Grant Young born.

" 27*th.*—Mrs. Eliza C. Palmer, wife of George Palmer, of Nantucket, died of consumption.

" 28*th.*—Edward Quintal (second) fell from the precipice upon the rocks below, and badly fractured his leg.

" *Dec.* 24*th.*—Charles William Grant born, son of the master of a whaler, whose wife had been left on the island.

" 1851, *Jan.* 1*st.*—Thursday O. Christian elected chief magistrate. John Buffett, jun., and Thomas Buffett, councillors.

" 8*th.*—Mary Anne M'Coy born.

" 21*st.*—Frances Adelaide Quintal born.

" 23*d.*—Observed the anniversary of the settlement of the colony. David Buffett and Martha Young married.

" *March* 15*th.*—By the accidental discharge of a fowling-piece in a whale-boat that was out fishing, three persons, viz. Abraham Quintal, John Buffett, and Fletcher Nobbs, were seriously injured.

" 30*th.*—Anna Rose Christian died, aged three years.

" *April* 27*th.*—Mary Isabel Adams born.

" *July* 13*th.*—Fairfax Moresby Quintal born.

" *August* 5*th.*—Joseph A. M. Buffett born.

" 10*th.* — Jacob Christian and Nancy Quintal married.

" 16*th.*—Twelve of the inhabitants sailed in the *Joseph Meigs* for the purpose of visiting Elizabeth Island. On their arrival at the island they discovered a human skeleton; and as nothing could be found that may lead to discover who this unfortunate individual was, it must remain a mystery.

" *Sept.* 5*th.*—Thomas A. Buffett born.

" 15*th.*—Julia E. Quintal born.

" *Oct.* 17*th.* — Leonard E. W. Christian born.

" 28*th.*—William Ward Dillon Adams born.

" *Nov.* 5*th.*—Sarah Clara Quintal born.

" 9*th.*—Julia Anna Christian born.

" 11*th.*—Thirty-eight of the inhabitants sailed in the ship *Sharon*, of Fairhaven, for the purpose of visiting Elizabeth Island. On Friday, 14th, after a boisterous passage of three days, they landed upon Elizabeth Island, when they immediately set about wooding the ship, and exploring the country, which is evidently of coral formation. The soil is very scanty, and totally unfit for cultivation. Various specimens of marine shells are dispersed all over the surface of the island, which, in combination with the thickly scattered pieces of coral, renders travelling both difficult and dangerous. Water is found on the north-west part of the island slowly dripping from the roof of a cave, which cannot be reached without the aid of ropes. The island rises about sixty feet above the level of the sea. Eight human skeletons were also found upon the island, lying in caves. They were doubtless the remains of some unfortunate shipwrecked seamen, as several pieces of a wreck were found upon the shore.

"27*th.*—Sarah Adams died from a disease of the spine, aged fifty-five years.

"*Dec.* 13*th.*—Philip M'Coy and Sarah Quintal, Benjamin Buffett and Eliza Quintal, married.

"1852, *Jan.* 2*d.*—Abraham B. Quintal elected chief magistrate; Frederick Young and David Buffett councillors.

"7*th.*—At about 1 P.M. intelligence was brought to the village that Robert (a native of one of the Society Islands, and who was left here sick from the American whale-ship *Balœna*) was washed from off the rocks by the surf; those who were at hand when the news was told, immediately hastened to the place to learn the truth of the statement. Upon arriving there, and not seeing anything of him, search was made along the rocks. This also proving unsuccessful, some of the men went in their canoes to search for him outside of the rocks. A few minutes after the canoes were launched, his hat was found some thirty or forty yards from the rocks. Being convinced from this that the man was drowned, the search was continued with renewed vigour, and, about an hour after, his body was seen lying at the bottom, in about seven fathoms of water, and about twenty yards from where he was washed off. The men succeeded in recovering the body, which was interred the same evening. It is but justice to the memory of this poor man to add, that his good and quiet behaviour while among us, had gained for him the esteem and good-will of all upon the island, and that his untimely end is deeply regretted by the whole community.

"*29th.*—At break of day a ship was reported close in with the shore; all who had turned out of their beds hastened to the edge of the precipice to ascertain the truth of the statement. Scarcely had they done so, when, from the heraldic bearing of her colours, she was by the teacher pronounced to be a man-of-war. The whale-boat was immediately manned, and in the course of a few hours she returned to shore, bringing with them Captain Wellesley, and others of the officers of H. M. ship *Dædalus*, from the Sandwich Islands, *viâ* Tahiti, bound to Valparaiso. Captain Wellesley and his officers remained on shore all night, and returned on board the following morning, when a fresh party landed from the ship. Captain Wellesley and his officers were pleased to express their approbation of what they saw upon the island, and have, by the urbanity of their conduct during the few hours they were with us, gained the good-will and esteem of all the inhabitants.

"30*th.*—Emily W. Christian born.

"31*st.*—At half-past seven this morning Captain Wellesley and his officers returned on board, and the *Dædalus* left this for Valparaiso, bearing the good wishes of the island.

"*March 7th.*—David R. B. Young born.

"14*th.*—David R. B. Young died, aged seven days.

"*April 5th.*—Fletcher Christian died, after a lingering illness of many months' duration, aged forty years. As a member of the community, the conduct of Fletcher Christian was ever worthy of imitation; suffice it to say, that his many amiable and agreeable qualities will cause his memory long to be cherished by those he has left behind.

"*June* 13*th.*—John F. Young born."

The following returns of births, deaths, and marriages, and some other particulars, from the year 1839 to the year 1852, inclusive, have been drawn chiefly from the authentic statements in the Register of the

Island, and partly from a report made by Captain Worth, of the *Calypso*, Sept. 27, 1848:—

"1837.—Births, 7; death, 1.

"1838.—Births, 5; death, 1.

"1839.—Births, 6; death, 1: 106 inhabitants; 53 males, 53 females: 52 scholars attend the public school.

"1840.—Births, 2; death, 0: 108 inhabitants; 53 males, 55 females: 51 scholars attend school, 58 the Sunday-school.

"1841.—Births, 7; deaths, 3; marriages, 0: inhabitants, 111: males, 54; females, 57: 50 scholars attend the Sunday-school.

"1842.—Births, 3; deaths, 2: males, 53; females, 59; total, 112: 50 children attend Sunday-school.

"1843.—Births, 6; deaths, 2; marriages, 0: males, 59; females, 60; total, 119: 20 males and 21 females eligible to vote.

"1844.—Births, 5; deaths, 0; marriages, 2: males, 60; females, 61: 24 males, 28 females eligible for voting at the Magistrate's election: 44 children attend the school.

"1845.—Births, 7; deaths, 0; marriages, 2: males, 65; females, 62; total, 127: 51 children attend the school.

"1846.—Births, 7; death, 1; marriages, 0: males, 69; females, 65; total, 134: 47 children attend public school.

"1847.—Births, 6; deaths, 0; marriages, 0: males, 72; females, 68; total, 140: 48 children attend the school.

"1848.—Births, 7; death, 1; marriages, 3: males, 74; females, 72; total, 146: 44 children attend the school; 30 scholars, of 14 years old and upwards, attend the Sunday-school. The attendance at the Wednesday Bible-class for adults quite satisfactory.

"1849.—Births, 10; death, 1; marriage, 1: males, 76; females, 79; total, 155: 47 children attend the school, 30 the Sunday-school.

"1850.—Births, 4; deaths, 3; marriage, 1: inhabitants, 156: males, 79; females, 76. Number of ships touching here, 47: American, 29; English, 17; Hanoverian, 1.

"1851.—Births, 12; deaths, 2; marriages, 3: inhabitants, 166; 81 females, and 85 males. Number of ships touching here, 24: American, 18; English, 6.

"1852.—The number of inhabitants is now 170: 88 males; 82 females."

The vessels mentioned in this work, which

have touched at Pitcairn's Island, between 1808 and 1853, inclusive, are as follow:—

VESSEL.	CAPTAIN.	DATE.	PAGE
Topaz	Folger	1808	90
H.M.S. Briton	Sir T. Staines	1814	113
H.M.S. Tagus	Pipon	1814	113
Sultan	Reynolds	1817	248
Elizabeth	Douglass	——	171
H.M.S. Blossom	Beechey	1825	124
Lovely	Blythe	1826	248
H.M.S. Seringapatam	Waldegrave	1830	130
Lucy Anne	J. Curry	1831	133
Bordeaux Packet	——	1831	249
H.M.S. Comet	Sandilands	1831	133
H.M.S. Challenger	Fremantle	1833	138
H.M.S. Actæon	Lord E. Russell	1837	176
H.M.S. Imogene	H. W. Bruce	1837	176
H.M.S. Fly	R. Elliott	1838	250
H.M.S. Sparrowhawk	Shepherd	1839	250
H.M.S. Curaçoa	Jenkin Jones	1841	155
Cyrus	J. Hall	1841	248
H.M.S. Talbot	Sir T. Thompson, Bt.	1843	251
America	——	1843	251
H.M.S. Basilisk	H. Hunt	1844	195
H.M.S. Spy	Wooldridge	1847	179
H.M.S. Calypso	Worth	1848	{ 32 190
H.M.S. Pandora	T. Wood	1849	149
H.M.S. Daphne	Fanshawe	1849	139
Fanny	Leathart	1849	142
Colonist	Marshall	1850	166
Noble	Parker	1850	164
H.M.S. Cockatrice	Dillon	1851	190
Joseph Meigs	——	1851	265
Sharon	——	1851	265
Balæna	——	1852	267
H.M.S. Dædalus	Wellesley	1852	268
H.M.S. Portland	Admiral Moresby	1852	206
Adeline Gibbs	Weeks	1852	215
H.M.S. Virago	Prevost	1853	273

About 330 vessels have touched at Pitcairn since 1808.

It will be seen that the last vessel mentioned on the foregoing list, is the *Virago.* In connexion with her visit to the island, it now becomes a painful duty to record a melancholy accident, which occurred at Pitcairn, towards the end of January last, and which must have spread a gloom over the small, but united band of friends, in whose welfare and happiness so many sympathise. The account cannot be given in any words so well as those of the Rev. W. H. Holman, their pastor, teacher, and medical friend, in Mr. Nobbs's absence.

It was stated at page 95, that the *Virago* had left Callao for Pitcairn on an errand of kindness. Some of her officers and crew had visited the island, and were about to sail, on their return, when Mr. Holman wrote :—

"January 29th, 1853.

"Captain Prevost had wished all good-bye, and gone on board the *Virago*, to start for Tahiti, when there occurred one of the most awful accidents that have ever taken place on the island. The magistrate, Matthew M'Coy, and two others, went to load an old gun that had been in the *Bounty*, to salute the *Virago*, on her departure. It appears that the rammer he used was an old rafter, on the top of which was a nail. While in the act of ramming home the powder, the friction caused by the nail effected the explosion of the powder. Matthew was blown away, several yards from the gun, and his arm knocked to pieces. The two others were severely wounded, together with an awful shock to all of them. I was at my house at the time, having just dined, and ran down, thinking it was the *Virago's* gun fired, as a farewell. Of course I found out what it was; and, by the time I got them conveyed to the nearest house, the surgeons of the steamer arrived.

"After two or three hours, Matthew's arm was amputated, and the doctor said, if he recovered the shock he would do very well; but I am sorry to say, that, after lingering eight hours in great agony, though sensible, he died. He was not only one of the best men on the island, but, I am happy to say, one of the best prepared for death. The other two, though severely hurt, are going on favourably, and, I trust, will recover.

"The poor widow is in great distress. She has seven children, and expects another in about five months. One hundred and thirty-five dollars, or twenty-seven pounds English money, were subscribed by the officers and crew of the *Virago;* and she will be well taken care of by the islanders. The gun has been spiked, to prevent further accidents."

This mournful news had not reached Mr. Nobbs, when he quitted Valparaiso; nor, in all probability, will he have been made acquainted with the sad intelligence, until his arrival at Pitcairn. In this case, the event must have given a tinge of sorrow to a meeting which was anticipated with so much joy. However, man proposeth, but God disposeth: and of this the disciplined minds of the islanders are well aware.

Matthew McCoy was a grandson of William McCoy, the mutineer, and was about 35 years of age. He was married to Margaret Christian, a sister of Mrs. Nobbs, and had a large family.

CHAPTER IX.

SERMON PREACHED BY MR. NOBBS IN THE ISLAND—THE HARP OF PITCAIRN.

THE reader will be glad of the opportunity of seeing some specimens of discourses preached in the distant island of Pitcairn to the descendants of the mutineers of the *Bounty*. It is pleasing to observe, from the faithful and affectionate tone of address adopted by the Preacher of Pitcairn towards the little flock assembled in the church of that place, that they have the blessed means of learning what is the faith and duty of a Christian. It will also be seen, that these extracts, as well as some poetical ones which follow, possess a certain degree of literary merit, independently of the peculiar interest of their source.

The following sermon was preached by Mr. Nobbs in the Church at Pitcairn:—

"Rev. xxii. 17.—*The Spirit and the Bride say, Come. And let him that heareth say, Come. And let him that is athirst come. And whosoever will, let him take the water of life freely.*

"There is in the Holy Scriptures such an adaptation to the wants of man as a mortal, and a sinner, that independent of the command to 'search' them, we ought to make the Bible 'the man of our counsel.' In all conditions of life, in prosperity or adversity, in sickness or health, in all places and at all times, the Bible, if referred to with a single eye and a prayerful disposition, will prove 'a lamp to our feet and a light to our paths.'

"Such considerations as these ought to stimulate us in our inquiries after happiness, even if it ended with this life; but if we believe that our time of sojourning here is merely probationary, and to be viewed only as an introduction into another and eternal state, yet that our everlasting happiness or misery depends entirely upon the use we make of the very short period allotted to us in the flesh, then are we not inexcusable if we neglect those means which God, of his infinite mercy and goodness, has been pleased to put within our reach?—the only means which, by the divine blessing, can make us wise unto salvation: for 'faith,' we are assured, 'cometh by hearing, and hearing by the word of God.' Open the Bible, and you can scarcely look upon a page that does not inform you of our wretched state by nature, and by actual transgression. It asserts that 'by one man's transgression many were made sinners;' that 'the heart of man is deceitful above all things, and desperately wicked;' and it declares in unequivocal language, 'The soul that sinneth, it shall die.' Dreadful as this view of the subject may appear,—and dreadful it really is to the impenitent offender,—yet, blessed be God! wherever in his holy word He has pronounced a curse against sin, an offer of pardon to the sinner, if he will turn from his evil way, invariably follows. So far from desiring the death of a sinner, God hath declared, 'It is because he is God, and not man, therefore we are not consumed.' And again, 'O Israel, thou hast destroyed thyself; but in me is thy help.' But, though numberless exceedingly precious promises for the encouragement of the 'weary and heavy-laden' are to be found in the Old Testament, yet it is in the life and death of Jesus Christ that all the promises of his Father are fully developed; for they are all 'Yea and Amen' in Christ Jesus our Lord; 'For God so loved the world, that He gave his only-begotten Son, that whosoever believeth in Him should not perish, but have everlasting life.' How encouraging then the thought that we have an Advocate with the Father—a compassionate High-Priest, who died for our sins, and rose again for our justification, who ever liveth to make intercession for us; and who now urgeth us by his word and by his Spirit to repent and be converted, that our sins may be blotted out! May we be made 'willing in the day of his power,' even now, while we consider the importance of the words in the text, in which we have:—

"1. *An exhortation.* 'The Spirit and the Bride say, Come.'

"2. *A command.* 'Let him that heareth say, Come.'

"3. *An encouragement.* 'Let him that is athirst come.'

"4. *A general invitation.* 'Whosoever will, let him take the water of life freely.'

"1. An exhortation. 'The Spirit and the Bride say, Come.'

"Our blessed Saviour said to his disciples, a short time before he suffered, 'It is expedient for you that I go away: for if I go not away, the Comforter will not come unto you.' And it is recorded in the Acts of the Apostles, that on the day of Pentecost, the Holy Ghost, the Comforter, descended upon the Apostles, and so endued them with power from on high, that, regardless of personal safety, they hastened forth into the midst of Jerusalem, and there, surrounded by a mixed and innumerable multitude, declared the wonderful works of God.

"But the Holy Spirit did not descend upon the Apostles merely to invest them with miraculous power, by which they might prove that Jesus was the Messiah, and that they, in consequence of their attachment to Him, while He sojourned upon earth, were thus singularly and favourably noticed. Far otherwise: for one especial purpose of the coming of the Holy Ghost was to 'convince the world of sin.' And that this purpose was accomplished on the memorable day alluded to is certain; for the multitude, after hearing Peter's declaration, 'were pricked in their heart, and said unto Peter, and to the rest of the apostles, Men and brethren, what shall we do?'

"Oh what a glorious specimen of divine mercy was here! what a proof that God is long-suffering, slow to anger, and willeth not the death of a sinner, but that all should turn unto Him, and live! Here, in the very place where Christ was crucified, among those who demanded his blood, did the Holy Spirit commence his operations, and say to each one of them, 'Come.' Brethren, we, by nature and practice, are exactly in the same state in which those Jews were. 'In us, that is, in our flesh, dwelleth no good thing.' But that same Holy Spirit who pricked the Jews in the heart is now striving with us, and convinces us, as it did them, of sin. It is allowed that the miraculous gifts of the

Spirit have ceased long since, but his ordinary operations in the heart of man are continued, and will continue till the great and notable day of the Lord come. But how do we treat them? Do we encourage them? Do we desire that they may be increased within us in frequency and power? Do we pray to be 'endued with the grace of the Holy Spirit, to amend our lives according to God's holy word?' Or when, in effect, He says to us, 'Come, now, and let us reason together,' do we resist his gracious influences and say, 'Depart from us, we desire not the knowledge of thy ways?' If, alas! this is the case, and that which the holy martyr Stephen said of the Jews, 'Ye stiffnecked and uncircumcised in heart and ears, ye do always resist the Holy Ghost,' is applicable to us, then 'there remaineth nothing but a certain fearful looking for of judgment and fiery indignation.' For the Almighty, whom we have insulted, will say unto us, 'Because I have called, and ye refused; I have stretched out my hand, and no man regarded; but ye have set at nought all my counsel, and would none of my reproof: I also will laugh at your calamity, I will mock when your fear cometh; when your fear cometh as desolation, and your destruction cometh as a whirlwind; when distress and anguish cometh upon you.'

"But there is another thing to be observed in this exhortation, viz. 'the BRIDE says, Come.' It is by this endearing appellation that Christ condescends to call the Church, that is, the congregation of the faithful in all ages up to the present time—wherever their lot may be cast, whatever their situation in life. The constant theme of their conduct and conversation to those around is—'We are journeying unto the place of which the Lord said, I will give it you; come thou with us, and we will do thee good, for the Lord hath spoken good concerning Israel.'

"When Peter exhorted the alarmed Jews to repent, the members of the visible Church were few in number, and oppressed with poverty; but did they on this account consider themselves excused from declaring the whole counsel of God, and making known the great salvation which had been effected by the death of the Lord Jesus? Certainly not. And what was the result? Multitudes of bigoted Jews alarmed, and at least three thousand souls added to the Church. Well might St. Paul exclaim, at a somewhat later period, 'God hath chosen the foolish things of the world to confound the wise, and God hath chosen the weak things of the world to confound the things that are mighty.' But time would fail me were I to attempt describing a millionth part of what the Bride has been ever ready to do, for the honour of her Beloved. Let it suffice to say, every individual under this roof has been invited by her to come unto the Lord.

"The valuable presents, of a religious kind, which have, from time to time, been sent to the distant island in which my lot is cast, are just so many invitations from the Church of Christ, saying, 'Come with us, and we will do thee good.' The Bibles, Prayer-books, sermons, tracts, and a variety of other good books which have been liberally bestowed upon us, all join in expressing the desire of their donors, 'Save yourselves from this untoward generation.' And, blessed be God! the invitation has been accepted. The benevolent call has been responded to: 'Thy people shall be my people, and thy God my God.' My brethren, we live in a glorious time. Never before was there such a simultaneous movement made against the power of darkness. Multitudes who, a few years since, had never heard of a Saviour, now have the glad tidings of salvation by Jesus Christ preached, every nation in their own language. And tens of thousands from distant lands and isles of the sea, are still stretching out their hands, and saying to the Church of Christ, 'Come over and help us.' Nor will they call in vain. Every year many holy men leave their country and friends to endure persecution, famine, nakedness, and encounter even death itself, to unstop the deaf ears, to open the blind eyes, to turn the heathen from the power of Satan unto God, that they may receive the forgiveness of sins, and inheritance among them which are sanctified by faith in Jesus Christ. 'This is the Lord's doing, and it is wonderful in our eyes.'

"2. A command. 'Let him that heareth say, Come.'

"Our blessed Saviour knew very well that the Church collectively, as a body, would always be anxious for the salvation of sinners, inasmuch as thereby the glory of her Lord would be eminently exalted. But He also foresaw that individual members of that Church would be prone to lukewarmness in his cause, and bury their talent in the earth. To prevent this, He says in the text, 'Let him that heareth say, Come.' As if He had said, 'Ye profess to be my disciples—to have received the remission of your sins through faith in my blood, which was shed for many. Do not, then, desire to keep so great a salvation for *yourselves* only, or for a few of your nearest and dearest relations. It was not my design, when I left the bosom of my Father and came down upon earth, to die for the sins of any particular kindred, or tongue, or nation of mankind: my blood was shed for all the sons of Adam, that as there is none other name under heaven given among men whereby they must be saved, and as my Father desireth not the death of a sinner, but that all should turn unto him and live—so whosoever cometh to him by me shall not perish, but have everlasting life. Publish, then, abroad this great salvation. Declare unto sinners what I have done for thy soul; tell them that although they have destroyed themselves, yet in me there is help—that you have found joy and peace in believing, and a good hope, through grace, to enable you to go on your way rejoicing.'

"This, my friends, appears to be the purport of that part of the text now under consideration; and, if correct, does it not loudly say to every sincere professor—'Up and be doing, that the Lord may be with thee?' Barren fig-trees will not be permitted to stand in Christ's vineyard. We should be instant, in season and out of season, exhorting with all long-suffering, never weary of our work of faith and labour of love; but should strive by word and deed to convince sinners of their danger, that they may turn from their evil ways. Thus doing, we shall comply with the commands of our Master, procure for ourselves an increase of happiness, and illustrate the promise of the Apostle, that 'he which converteth a sinner from the evil of his ways, shall save a soul from death, and hide a multitude of sins.'

"3. Encouragement. 'Let him that is athirst come.'

"It is one of the glorious attributes of the

Gospel that a sincere reception of it renders null and void all the denunciations of the Law. For whosoever has fled to it as 'the shadow of a great rock in a dry and weary land,'—whosoever is subjected to its salutary influences, is 'no longer under the law, but under grace.' The awakened sinner may write bitter things against himself, but to such an one it may be said, 'Be of good cheer, *He* calleth thee.' Jesus was fully aware of the obstacles that would arise in the way of a penitent sinner. He knew also that, as no one would flee from the wrath to come without his suggesting the necessity, so no one could escape but by his special assistance. He has, therefore, cheered the road from death unto life with encouragements and consolations. Let us, then, for the benefit of the thirsty soul, recite two or three of them. They are the words of the blessed Jesus himself—'There is joy in the presence of the angels of God over one sinner that repenteth.' 'Come unto me, all ye that labour and are heavy laden, and I will give you rest.' 'I am the bread of life: he that cometh to me shall never hunger, and he that believeth on me shall never thirst.' 'Him that cometh unto me I will in nowise cast out.' 'Whatsoever ye shall ask in my name, that will I do, that my Father may be glorified in me. If ye shall ask anything in my name, I will do it.' Are not these rills exceedingly delicious to the parched, fainting soul? Ye that hunger and thirst after righteousness, declare, is it not such consolation as this that ye have need of? Yes, you may reply, if I were included, such inviting language would cheer my heart: my sincere desire is, to be admitted into Christ's fold: but I am so laden with sin, my corruptions are so many, I am so vile in my own eyes, and consequently must be so much more vile in His sight who is of purer eyes than to behold iniquity, that my heart faileth, and I know not wherewith to come before the Most High.—O thou of little faith, wherefore dost thou doubt? Is not obedience better than sacrifice? What is it that Christ requires of thee, but that thou shouldst close with his unqualified offer of free salvation? If thou comest to Him polluted, He will cleanse thee; if thou art naked, He will clothe thee; if thou art wretched, He will cheer thee. He will give thee joy for sorrow, riches for poverty, health for sickness. To sum up the whole, come to Christ without delay. While the Spirit worketh within you, speak to Him in earnest, persevering prayer, and He will hear your supplications: you may remain in heaviness for a time; but be not weary in well-doing, and the certain result will be that He will speak comfort to thy soul. He will enlighten thy mind, and bid thee 'go in peace, thy sins are forgiven.'

"4. A general invitation. 'Whosoever will, let him take the water of life freely.'

"Glory be to God! salvation by Jesus Christ is so fully made known, and so frankly offered in the Gospel, that whosoever will, may take the water of life freely. Nor is the invitation confined to Gospel time. Long before Christ appeared in the flesh, the proclamation was extant. Hear the prophet Isaiah, under the influence of the Holy Spirit, crying aloud—'Ho, every one that thirsteth, come ye to the waters, and he that hath no money; come ye, buy, and eat; yea, come, buy wine and milk without money and without price.' Again—' Seek ye the Lord while he may be found, call upon him while he is near: let the wicked forsake his way, and the unrighteous man his thoughts: and let him return unto the Lord, and he will have mercy upon him; and to our God, for he will abundantly pardon.' Hear also what God saith by the mouth of the prophet Ezekiel—' Have I any pleasure at all in the death of the wicked, and not that he should return from his ways, and live? As I live, saith the Lord, I have no pleasure in the death of the wicked, but that the wicked turn from his ways and live: turn ye, turn ye from your evil ways; for why will ye die?' Here are no exceptions made; God willeth not the death of a sinner. He says to no one, Thou art condemned from eternity; but contrariwise, ' Turn ye, turn ye; why will ye die?'

" John the Baptist testified of Christ that He was 'the Lamb of God which taketh away the sins of the world.' And the Lord himself said to his disciples—' If I be lifted up, I will draw all men unto me.'

" My object in reciting these passages of

Scripture is, to illustrate the great Scripture truth, that God will accept the returning penitent; and that, while the day of salvation lasts, we are encouraged to come unto Him that 'willeth not the death of a sinner, but that all should turn to Him and live.'

"But let not this forbearance and long-suffering of God be perverted to our own ruin. '*Now* is the accepted time, now is the day of salvation.'"

This sermon was not only preached in Pitcairn's Island, but also in London. On Sunday morning, Nov. 28th, 1852, the Rev. G. H. Nobbs delivered the same discourse in the parish church of St. Dunstan in the East, City, and added the following passages:—

"And now, my brethren, will you bear with me for a few moments, whilst I refer to circumstances which have come in a great measure under my own immediate notice, in the community over which I have for nearly twenty-five years been the unworthy pastor?

"Many years ago, an officer and some seamen belonging to the British navy, after committing an unjustifiable act — that of mutiny—fled for safety to Pitcairn, an isolated rock in the South Pacific Ocean, taking with them some Otaheitan men and women. Within ten years, all the men, with the exception of two, came to an untimely end; one of these two died of consumption; and the last of this party of mutineers was left on the island with five or six heathen women, and twenty fatherless children. After some time, this man, John Adams by name, became seriously impressed with the responsibility of the situation in which he was placed. Here were a number of young persons, between the ages of five and fifteen years, growing up in ignorance of the God who made them. And they would, humanly speaking, in a few years have become confirmed idolaters, from the example of their heathen mothers.

"These considerations weighed heavily on Adams's mind; and it was then that he had two alarming dreams, which so affected him, that he could scarcely eat or sleep for some time; when he bethought himself of the Bible, brought on shore from the *Bounty,* which had been much used by Christian, and also by Young in his last illness. After some search he found it, and commenced reading it, imperfectly at first, for he had never been to school, but had taught himself what he did know from scraps of paper picked up by him, when a boy, in the streets of London. Being, however, a man of excellent natural abilities, he was soon enabled to read with facility, both the Bible, and the Book of Common Prayer; a single Prayer-book also having happily been recovered from the *Bounty*. He commenced praying in secret three times a day; nor did he pray in vain; his mind became enlightened, he saw his guilt and danger; and he was almost tempted to despair of pardon. Still, as he persevered in reading the Bible, he gradually became acquainted with the Gospel method of salvation; and, by the guidance of the Holy Spirit, was enabled to come to Him who is mighty to save. In short, my brethren, he was brought to Jesus.

"Now, mark the result. From this time he commenced instructing the children of the mutineers, first by reading to them portions of the Scriptures, and subsequently teaching them to read for themselves; and so anxious were the young people to learn, that on one occasion two of the lads, who were employed by Adams to make a mattock of iron from the wreck of the *Bounty*, instead of accepting the promised compensation, (a quantity of gunpowder,) told Adams, they would rather he should give them some extra lessons from God's Book, a name by which they used to designate the Bible. And now peace and contentment pervaded this rock of the West. The young men and women entered into the social relations of husband and wife; and they, in turn, depending on that most precious promise of their all-sufficient Saviour, 'Where two or three are gathered together in my name, there am I in the midst of them,' instructed their children with that knowledge which is better than riches. They brought them to Jesus.

"The population of this settlement now amounts to 170 persons, who are living without any dissensions, and with but one form of Church government—that of the Church of England. The Holy Bible, and the

Church Prayer-book, are their chief rules of guidance; their motto, 'One Faith, one Lord, one Baptism.' And when I, their pastor, took a sorrowful leave of them, about three months since, they were strong in faith, giving glory to God. That they, and all who hear me this day, may be included in that most precious invitation, 'Come, ye blessed of my Father, inherit the kingdom prepared for you from the foundation of the world,' may God of His infinite mercy grant, for Jesus Christ's sake. Amen."

The same sermon was preached by Mr. Nobbs in St. Mary's Chapel, Park Street, Grosvenor Square, on Sunday morning, December 12th, 1852, and was printed at the request of several members of the congregation.

On the occasion of a wedding sermon, preached by Mr. Nobbs in Pitcairn Church, four young persons having, on the same morning, entered into the holy estate of matrimony, he took his text from Eph. v. 22, &c. :—" Wives, submit yourselves unto your own husbands, as unto the Lord. For the husband is the head of the wife, even as Christ is the head of the Church: and he is the saviour of the body. Therefore as the Church is subject unto Christ, so let the wives be to their own husbands in everything. Husbands, love your wives, even as Christ also loved the Church, and gave himself for it."

After speaking of the holy influence of the Christian religion, in restoring women to their proper place in society, he described the ignominy with which females are treated, not only among the natives of the islands of the Southern Pacific, but among the Hindoos, and Mohammedans, and the inhabitants of other countries, especially in the East, in which a false religion, and absurd superstitions prevail. To this evil principle he attributed the custom, so long prevalent in India, of sacrificing widows at the funerals of their husbands, and wickedly destroying numbers of female infants.

"I am sure, my female friends, your hearts are ready to sink within you at the recital of such horrible atrocities; but it is the truth. Nay, I need only refer you to

U

the account of the land from whence your mothers and grandmothers came. You have heard them declare how the women were degraded in their country, being looked upon as inferior creatures, and how often female infants were put to death. So true is it, that the dark places of the earth are full of cruelty. But where the Christian religion obtains, there woman rises to her proper station—the friend of man. Nor are her expectations of happiness confined to this life. She is informed in the Scriptures, that she has an immortal soul, which Christ died to redeem, and that after death she will be eternally happy or miserable, as she employs the talent here committed to her care. She will understand, also, that, as the Church of which she is a member is required to be obedient to the commands of Christ, its Head, so must she also be obedient unto her husband, and for the same reason. Christ is the head of the Church, and the man is the head of the woman.

"How thankful ought every woman present to be when she reflects on the wonderful goodness of God in preserving the life of the late Mr. John Adams, until a knowledge of the Christian religion was extant among you. Had he been cut off when ye were in your childhood, in all probability, your husbands would be bowing to a stock or a stone, and ye, instead of uniting in the worship of the true God, would not indeed have been *permitted* to enter the temple of idols, but would have remained all your lives the slaves of sensuality and caprice; despised by your tyrannical masters, scorned by your own children, deserted in your sickness, and without hope, and without God in the world.

"Bless God, then, for Jesus Christ, my female friends. Serve Him with sincerity of heart, and remember it is He that commands you to submit yourselves unto your own husbands as unto himself.

"Men and brethren,—To you I next address my discourse. On you chiefly depends the happiness of your families. Remember, when you entered the married state, you promised to love and honour your wives. See, then, that you are true to your engagements. Let Christ's love to His Church be an ensample for you to copy. To each I would say, Love your wife with a pure heart, fervently. Never speak disrespectfully of her to other people. Never call her ill names; neither be fond of showing that you are master before other people. This makes a woman feel her inferiority, and lowers her in the opinion of many. Avoid all occasion of controversy in public. If you differ in opinion, argue the matter over by yourselves, and you will come to a rational conclusion sooner than in company. See that your children pay a proper respect to their mother. Set them a good example yourself, and they will be easily taught to follow it. Children are imitative beings; and if they observe one parent indulge in sarcasms, or improper expressions at the expense of the other, they will be sure to do so too. Many children have been taught to despise their mother from improper appellations bestowed upon her by their other parent. If your wife wishes to send the children to any place, never countermand her orders without good reason; and then tell her why you do so. Whenever your wife sees fit to chastise any of the children, do not interfere in their behalf. By so doing you teach them to set her authority at nought. But time would fail me, were I to attempt giving directions in every particular relative to the proper conduct of married persons towards each other, and towards their children. The Word of God abounds with instructions as to our mutual duties; I shall therefore conclude with this piece of advice.

"'Husbands, love your wives, and be not bitter against them;' 'live with them according to knowledge, for no man ever yet hated his own flesh; but nourisheth and cherisheth it, even as the Lord the Church.' 'Rejoice with the wife of thy youth, and be thou always satisfied with her love; for she is thy companion, and the wife of thy covenant.' 'Go not after a stranger; and let none deal treacherously against the wife of his youth.'

"'Wives, be in subjection to your own husbands; that, if any obey not the word, they also may without the word be won by the conversation of the wives; while they behold your chaste conversation coupled with fear.' 'For after this manner in the old time the holy women, who trusted in God, were in subjection to their own husbands: even as Sarah obeyed Abraham, calling him lord; whose daughters ye are, as long as ye do well.'

"And for your comfort and commendation, and to induce in you a deportment in conformity with the will of God, remember it is expressly said, 'A prudent wife is from the Lord. The heart of her husband doth safely trust in her; she will do him good and not evil all the days of her life. She openeth her mouth with wisdom; and in her tongue is the law of kindness. She looketh well to the ways of her household, and eateth not the bread of idleness. Her children arise up, and call her blessed; her husband also, and he praiseth her.'

"Husbands and wives excite each other in the path of duty. Form the holy resolution, that you and your house will serve the Lord; and having made this resolution, persevere in it till death. Be diligent in reading the Word of God, and causing it to be read in your families. 'Search the Scriptures, for in them ye think ye have eternal life,' is a precept of our blessed Lord; and parents are in a peculiar manner bound to instruct their children in the knowledge of the Word of God. Family prayer is a duty as absolutely necessary as reading the Word of God; for prayer is an excellent means to render reading effectual. We read that our blessed Lord, when He dwelt on earth, promised a peculiar blessing to joint supplications: 'Wheresoever two or three are gathered together in my name, there am I in the midst of them.' Add to this, that we are commanded by the Apostle to 'pray always with all manner of supplication,' which, doubtless, includes family prayer.

"Remember, the time will come, and that, perhaps, very shortly, when we must all appear before the judgment-seat of Christ, where we must give a solemn and strict account how we have had our conversation in our respective families in this world. How will you endure to see your children, who ought to be your joy and crown of rejoicing in the day of our Lord Jesus, coming out as so many swift witnesses against you! O consider this, all ye that forget to serve the Lord with your respective households, lest He pluck you away, and there be none to deliver you!

"Do, I beseech you, seriously reflect on what has been said this morning. It is the last day of the year; and who may be permitted to see the close of the approaching year, God only knows. Do but seriously and frequently reflect on, and act as persons that believe, such important truths, and you will not neglect either your own spiritual welfare, or your family's. And though, after all your pious endeavours, some may continue unreformed, yet you will have this comfortable reflection, that you did what you could to make your families religious, and therefore may rest assured of sitting down with Abraham, Isaac, Cornelius, Hannah, Lydia, Mary, and Dorcas, and all the godly families, who, in their several generations, shone forth as so many lights in their respective households upon earth. Now the Lord Jesus Christ, who is God over all, blessed for ever, assist and watch over you, and keep you from all evil and sin here, and present you before his Father faultless at the great day of account.

"To God the Father, the Lord Jesus Christ, and the blessed Spirit, three Persons, and one eternal God, be ascribed all honour, power, glory, might, majesty, and dominion, now, henceforth, and for ever. Amen."

As a suitable conclusion of this work, a few little poems, from the Pastor's pen, are inserted, by his permission, not at his request. These, being considered as simple strains of the Harp of Pitcairn, will not be subjected to severe criticism. On the contrary, the piety, loyalty, and evident desire for the happiness of others, which are manifested in the following lines, will commend them to the candid Christian reader. They may even tend, as an addition to what has appeared of their author in the foregoing pages, to excite a feeling of thankfulness that, in the course of God's providence, such a man should have been called to such a post, at the very time that a teacher and friend was most urgently needed by the islanders.

EVENING HYMN.

1.

FATHER, let our supplications
Find acceptance in thy sight;
Free from Satan's foul temptations,
From the perils of the night
O preserve us,
Till return of morning light.

2.

Jesus, friend of dying sinners,
Ere we close our eyes in sleep,
Let the hope that dwells within us
Prove thou dost thy people keep:
Gracious Shepherd!
From the wolf defend thy sheep.

3.

Holy Ghost, be ever near us,
Make our hearts thy blest abode;
Strengthen, purify, and cheer us,
Raise our waking thoughts to God;
With sweet visions
Gild the hours on sleep bestow'd.

4.

Father, Son, and Holy Spirit,
Us into thy keeping take;
Not for our deserts or merit,
Solely for thy mercy's sake,
O protect us,
When we sleep and when we wake.

HYMN.

1.

I WILL not encumber my verse
  With metaphor, figure, or trope;
Nor will I the praises rehearse
  Of aught in Creation's wide scope;
My Bible shall furnish the theme,
  My subject will angels applaud,
My soul shall rejoice in his name,
  My Brother, my Saviour, my God.

2.

My Brother, How grateful that sound
  When sorrow preys deep on the heart;
When malice and discord abound,
  What balm can a brother impart.
A tender, unchangeable friend,
  On whose bosom 'tis sweet to recline,
Ever prompt to assist or defend;—
  Such a Friend, such a Brother is mine.

3.

My Saviour! Thrice glorious name!
  But who of the children of men
The wondrous appointment may claim?
  Or who can the title sustain?
Immanuel, Jesus, alone
  Doth fulness and fitness combine,
He only for sin can atone,
  And He is my Saviour, e'en mine.

4.

My God! What a myst'ry is this;
Jehovah appears as a man!
Truth, wisdom, grace, mercy, and peace,
Devised the inscrutable plan;
He came to redeem us from hell,
He died to effect his design,
He reigns where the glorified dwell,
And he is my God, even mine.

5.

Then what upon earth need I fear?
My Brother partakes my distress,
My Saviour attends to my prayer,
My God deigns to pardon and bless.
Through life as I journey along,
Sustain'd by thy staff and thy rod,
Thy love shall give life to my song,
My Brother, my Saviour, my God.

Pitcairn's Island, South Pacific Ocean,
Lat. 25° 4′ Long. 130° 8′.

THE ANGEL'S LAMENT.

CONTRASTED WITH LUKE XV. 10.

1.

ENSLAVED by sin, in league with hell,
Prompt to obey, should Satan call,
Thine own deceivings please thee well;—
Opprest, yet held in willing thrall:

The gall of bitterness is thine,
  Still dost thou not thy state discern,
Though more degraded than the swine,
  Thou wilt not to thy home return.

2.

The Crown is fallen from thy head,
  The gold of Ophir, O how dim!
Burning appears in beauty's stead,
  And all thy garb in wretched trim.
Alas, alas! how art thou changed,
  Yet angels thy declensions mourn,
Though from thy Saviour-God estranged,
  He still invites thee to return.

3.

What is thy hope? What canst thou find
  To equal thy Redeemer's love?
Riches are fleeting as the wind,
  And pride and lust will adders prove.
Oh stay, Oh stay thy mad career,
  Ere to destruction thou art borne,
Infatuated sinner, hear,
  Deluded wanderer, return.

4.

Recal to mind those precious hours
  When in the truth thy footsteps trod;
When heart and mind and all thy powers
  Were dedicated to thy God.

Sweet, sweet it was to hear thee then,
In grateful strains to heaven upborne;
And shall they not ascend again—
O prodigal, return, return!

5.

Upon presumption's tottering mast,
Held by a thread in reckless sleep,
Thou fear'st not, though th' approaching blast,
May whirl thee headlong to the deep.
Awake, awake, nor longer dare
The vengeance thou affect'st to scorn,
Lest thy enraged Creator swear,
'*Thou never, never shalt return.*'

6.

Canst thou 'midst endless burnings dwell?
Or with eternal fire abide?
That thou wouldst madly doom to hell
Thy soul for which Immanuel died.
Arise, arise, repent, believe,
The Spirit's call no longer spurn,
Thy Saviour will the welcome give,
And angels joy at thy return.

This Hymn was composed at the request of several of our little community, who wished to have one of their own, which they might sing to the pathetic air of 'Bonny Doon.' G. H. N.

I BELIEVE, I BELIEVE.

"How are you to-day, Polly?" said I to the wife of George Adams, who had long been grievously afflicted with a cancer in her breast, and was rapidly approaching the grave.

"*I shall soon be at home, sir,*" she said.

"On whom is your hope placed at this time?" I asked.

"*On the blessed Saviour who died for me, and has redeemed me.*"

And then she went on to declare her faith and hope, of which the accompanying verses are the substance.

You ask how I feel in the prospect of death,
  And whether the grave has no terrors for me?
If bright are my hopes, and unshaken my faith,
  And to whom for relief in my sufferings I flee?
The questions are weighty, and I am so weak,
  Yet will I endeavour an answer to give;
And this is the substance of what I would speak,--
  I believe, I believe.

On the brink of the grave it has pleased my Lord
  To keep me long waiting the word to depart!
And though for dismission I oft have implored,
  Yet He has forgiven the thought of my heart:

Though often impatient and prone to complain,
  Much love in this chastening I plainly perceive,
Our Father afflicts not his children in vain;
  I believe, I believe.

This body so wasted by lingering disease,
  That scarce to the worms it can furnish a meal,
Insatiate death as a trophy may seize,
  And in me the sad fruits of transgression reveal:
But must I for ever continue his prey?
  No,—Jesus my dust from his grasp shall retrieve;
The call to arise I shall gladly obey;
  I believe, I believe.

I know, on this earth my Redeemer shall stand,
  And these eyes, though now dim, shall his glories behold;
My powers so reduced, shall with knowledge expand,
  And this heart throb with rapture, which now beats so cold:—
His voice I shall hear, and in accents divine,
  Shall I, then made worthy, a welcome receive;
In his presence to dwell 'twill for ever be mine;
  I believe, I believe.

This then is my hope; and I am not deceived,
  On the word of my God I can fully depend;
I know by the Spirit, on whom I've believed;
  That He will support and console to the end;—
Immanuel's death hath Jehovah appeased;
  That death on the cross did my ransom achieve;
That death is my passport when I am released:
  I believe, I believe; yes, I firmly believe.

Polly, wife of George Adams, departed this life December 17th, 1843, aged 48 years.

I have merely versified part of the foregoing conversation. It is in sum and substance a reply to an inquiry made by me concerning her state of mind in the prospect of death, which was then rapidly approaching. Assuredly, her end was peace.

George H. Nobbs,
Pastor and School-master.

SONG OF THE PITCAIRN ISLANDERS,

ON THE ANNIVERSARY OF THE BIRTHDAY OF QUEEN VICTORIA.

1.

The Queen! the Queen! our gracious Queen!
Come, raise on high your voices,
And let it by your smiles be seen
That every heart rejoices.
Her natal day we'll celebrate
With ardour and devotion,
And Britain's festal emulate
In the Pacific Ocean.

X

2.

Now let old England's flag be spread,
  That flag long-famed in story;
And as it waves above our head,
  We'll think upon its glory.
Then fire the gun, the *Bounty's* gun,
  And set the bell a-ringing,
And then, with hearts and voices one,
  We'll all unite in singing:

3.

The Queen! the Queen! God bless the Queen!
  And all her royal kindred;
Prolong'd and happy be her reign,
  By faction never hindered.
May high and low, the rich and poor,
  The happy or distressed,
O'er her wide realm, from shore to shore,
  Arise and call her blessed.

4.

Our friends, and oh! they love us well,
  Unnumber'd favours say so;
Our hearts are with them where they dwell,
  And first in Valparaiso;
New Zealand, Sydney, Hobart Town,
  And those upon their journey,
With many more already down
  In golden Californy.

5.

We've pass'd o'er some whom we respect,
  Of varied name and nation,
But not from coldness or neglect,
  Or want of inclination.
God bless them all, wherever seen,
  On ocean or on dry land,
Now give three cheers for Britain's Queen,
  And three for Pitcairn's Island.

Zeitfracht Medien GmbH
Ferdinand-Jühlke-Straße 7
99095 Erfurt, Deutschland
produktsicherheit@kolibri360.de